GARDENS of VANCOUVER

GARDENS OF

VANCOUVER

For Kurt Nielsen / Fellow Gardener

COLLIN VARNER & CHRISTINE ALLEN

PHOTOGRAPHY BY JOHN DOWELL

RAINCOAST BOOKS

Vancouver

First published in 1999 by

Raincoast Books
8680 Cambie Street
Vancouver, B.C.
V6P 6M9
(604) 323-7100

1   2   3   4   5   6   7   8   9   10

CANADIAN CATALOGUING IN PUBLICATION DATA

Allen, Christine.
  Gardens of Vancouver

  ISBN 1-55192-288-6

  1. Gardens—British Columbia—Vancouver.
  2. Gardening—British Columbia—Vancouver.
  I. Varner, Collin.
  II. Title.
  SB466.C32V32 1999   635'.09711'33   C99-910970-7

Printed in Hong Kong

Designed by Val Speidel
Cover photography by John Dowell

Raincoast Books gratefully acknowledges the support of the Government of Canada, through the Book Publishing Industry Development Program, the Canada Council and the Department of Canadian Heritage. We also acknowledge the assistance of the Province of British Columbia, through the British Columbia Arts Council.

CONTENTS

INTRODUCTION

*What, if anything, do the infinity of traditional and individual ideas
of a garden have in common? They vary so much in purpose, in size, in
style and content that not even flowers, or even plants at all, can be
said to be essential. In the last analysis, there is only one common
factor between all gardens, and that is control by man. Control, that is,
for aesthetic reasons. A garden is not a farm.*

—HUGH JOHNSON, *The Principles of Gardening*

*I*N THE BEGINNING THERE WAS THE
wilderness. Along Burrard Inlet, a
deep, gloomy rainforest was both the
raison d'être for the first lumbering
community there and a hostile environment holding back settlement. The
native communities clustered along
waterways at natural grassy clearings:
Mahli, near the mouth of the Fraser
River, was a permanent settlement, as
was Sun'ahk at the mouth of False
Creek, while other sites, such as
Ee'yull-mough, now known as Jericho, functioned as
seasonal fishing camps.

When the first European settlers arrived on the
shores of Burrard Inlet in the early 1860s and began
pushing back against the rainforest, they were more
concerned with levelling the landscape than with culti-
vating it. The first farmers, the McRoberts, the

McCleerys and the Magees, avoided
the problem of the rainforest alto-
gether by settling on the natural
meadows along the Fraser River, on
what is now Sea Island and, on the
Vancouver side, Southlands. Another
early settler was William Mackie
who, on May 8, 1882, planted a garden in a logged-off clearing at what is
now Douglas Park, east of Oak Street
at about 20th Avenue. Alas, the seeds
he had with him yielded only cab-
bages and onions. Gardening in Vancouver for aesthetic
purposes, as distinct from farming, had to await the
arrival of a middle class.

And so the history of gardening in Vancouver dates
back little more than a century, when the coming of the
Canadian Pacific Railway in 1887 brought with it an influx of executives and businessmen—people of means

and some leisure, who built the first exclusive residential district along West Hastings Street and surrounded their commodious homes with gardens and glass-roofed conservatories. Respectability in the robust little mill town included fashioning the houses and streets in a style reflective of eastern Canada, and thus when plank sidewalks were laid along "Blueblood Alley," as it was then dubbed, the first boulevard plantings were mountain ash and broad-leafed maple, two of the few native deciduous trees.

To the new arrivals, everything about the west-coast flora was strange. Thousands of miles from home, they sought out the familiar, and eagerly patronized any business that imported seeds from England or eastern Canada. Books and pamphlets reproduced artists' impressions of English gardens, reminders of home for settlers in an alien landscape of towering fir and cedar. Privet hedges, hawthorns and lilacs were popular, neat young conifers dotted expanses of lawn, rambler roses nodded over porches. Among the less well-heeled, in their modest wood-frame houses in the new districts carved by logging and land-clearing, the urge to stencil a familiar pattern over the slash and tree stumps expressed itself in little plots of dahlias and a struggling rosebush or two.

Soon, a gardening community emerged. One of the most enthusiastic gardeners in the 1890s was B.T. Rogers, the owner of the B.C. Sugar Refinery, who traded palms with Lord Mount Stephen in Montreal, swapped a banana plant for $2.50 worth of cyclamen and entertained the Duke of Westminster's gardener on a February day in 1896 shortly after he had pruned his roses. Julia Henshaw, having published *Mountain Wildflowers of Canada* in 1906, moved to Caulfeild in West Vancouver and together with a group of Anglophiles established a "little Cornish village" of winding lanes and rockeries. Another Englishman, W.H. Malkin, established his Southlands estate on South West Marine Drive

around 1910, and developed the grounds with perennial borders, a rose garden and conservatory, espaliered fruit trees, a vegetable garden and greenhouses.

A number of different styles began to develop. There were adherents of the formal garden, like Colonel and Mrs. A.D. McRae, both Ontarians, who built their neoclassical mansion, Hycroft, on the Shaughnessy slopes, and were soon importing unusual plants for its garden, such as the Deodar cedar which now dominates the southern aspect. Another strong influence came from southern California, home of the so-called "Pasadena lifestyle" that was widely publicized through bungalow books and mass-market magazines such as *Sunset*. One proponent was the architect Thomas Fee, whose 1907 home on Gilford Street in the West End featured a pair of Chusan palms flanking the entranceway. At the same time, a block away on the edge of the beach, the lifeguard Joe Fortes was responding to the charms of the classic English cottage garden, enveloping his little clapboard dwelling with honeysuckle and filling its tiny front garden with shrub roses.

During the prosperous 1920s, landscape designers such as Arthur Robillard, who had supervised the development of the quarry garden at the Butchart property on Vancouver Island in 1913, and his son, Raoul, were in demand to apply their skills to estates in Shaughnessy, West Vancouver and along South West Marine Drive overlooking the Fraser River delta. The rockery garden at Oakherst on 58th Avenue near Oak Street, developed by the Maitland family, was dramatic enough to attract the Kodak company, which chose it in the 1930s to demonstrate the capabilities of its new colour film. During the Second World War, the concept of gardens as fundraisers got its start in Vancouver when the local war bond committee arranged "Gardens Beautiful" tours, providing the general public with their first opportunity to see the city's big private gardens and absorb the ideas of the tastemakers.

"Everything that slows us down and forces patience, everything that sets us back into the slow cycles of nature is a help. Gardening is an instrument of grace." —May Sarton

After the war, the influx of returning veterans and immigrants populated new subdivisions springing up across the city, and a new generation of homeowners established suburban gardens around their suburban bungalows.

Some definable ethnic styles emerged, notably the statuary, bright annuals, paving, pots and 'Queen Elizabeth' roses around the "Vancouver Specials" of Italian families on the east side of the city. On some blocks, every homeowner had his hydrangea. Along the Stanley Park causeway, 60,000 daffodil bulbs were planted, the gift of a grateful Dutch government to their Canadian liberators.

Most significantly, however, the postwar years saw the beginnings of a shift in attitude among Vancouver gardeners from defying the wilderness to accommodating it and, in recent years with the influence of the environmental movement, to revering it. Rose gardens, bedding schemes and rows of dahlias were still popular, but an increasing number of residents, especially on the slopes of the North Shore mountains, were resisting the urge to clearcut their land; instead, encouraged by landscape designers like the Robillards and architects such as Ron Thom, Arthur Erickson and Wolfgang Gerson, they fitted their houses and their gardens into the rugged landscape, planting rhododendrons among the evergreens and carpeting the ground with ferns and native groundcovers that took happily to the shade and the damp, peaty soil. For the first time, the interrelationship of the house and the garden became a significant component of the west-coast style.

As these changes took place in private gardens, public gardens emerged, or metamorphosed from earlier incarnations, to offer an equally diverse spectrum.

Vancouver is rich in parks, yet the majority of them remain primarily strolling places and playgrounds rather than gardens. Unique features distinguish one or two, such as the red and white horse chestnut trees laid out in the shape of the Union Jack which grace Victoria Park in North Vancouver, or the collection of unusual trees that make the centre of The Crescent in Shaughnessy Heights a mini arboretum. A few parks are significant for the vestiges of a historic landscape they contain, among them Maple Grove Park in Kerrisdale with its grove of mighty tree stumps and Tatlow Park in Kitsilano, where a natural creek still runs above ground. Only Lighthouse Park in West Vancouver retains a last untouched piece of wilderness: a narrow track to the lighthouse and a clutch of rustic buildings, a few well-trodden trails, a plaque or two are the only infringements on its pristine landscape of tall trees and undergrowth.

For gardeners who seek inspiration from the kind of pleasing design or wealth of flowers, shrubs and trees to be found in private gardens, the choice is small but rewarding, with the city's two botanical gardens leading the way. The older of these by more than 50 years, the University of British Columbia Botanical Garden, was established in 1916. Divided by the road that sweeps around the university peninsula, the garden reveals two distinctly different faces. On the Fraser River side, a forest landscape is cut by trails and interplanted with vines, shade-loving plants and a collection of 5,000 rhododendrons. On the other, there are demonstration plots of vegetables and herbs framed by espaliered fruit trees, a rocky hillside of alpines from around the world, long perennial borders and a native bog garden of alder and maple, skunk cabbage, wild berry bushes and labrador tea. Behind a boxwood hedge, stone troughs laid out in neat rows hold tiny conifers, succulents and mats of thyme.

Also on the university peninsula and administered by UBC, Nitobe Memorial Garden occupies a triangular plot of land enclosed by a high wall and entered through a grove of tall trees underplanted with azaleas. A classic Japanese-style landscape of winding paths, mossy

glades, running water and glassy pools, it mingles west coast huckleberries and kinnikinnick with traditional irises and flowering cherries.

While the UBC gardens were carved out of forest settings, VanDusen Botanical Garden occupies the site of a former golf course, meeting the interesting challenge of transforming greens, fairways and sandtraps into a combination of appealing landscapes and authoritative botanical collections. Much of the credit for the result belongs to two men: Bill Livingstone, who laid

out the contours, and Roy Forster, curator of the garden from 1972 to 1997. Under their hands, the lakes, slopes and groves of trees have become the frame for a series of gardens defined by collections from the different continents or by a particular type of plant such as the rose collection, the meconopsis dell or the famous rhododendron walk.

To fulfill the garden's educational mandate, plants are labelled and strategic plaques explain the significance of certain collections or botanical curiosities. Rely-

ing on the appeal of permanent plantings rather than the impact of vast beds of seasonal colour, the philosophy at VanDusen reveals a sensibility much more in tune with the private gardener than most public gardens reflect.

Queen Elizabeth Park, which occupies the highest point of land in the city of Vancouver, is another example of a transformation from a former use. In this instance, a disused stone quarry and rabbit-infested hillside have become a display garden and arboretum surrounded by a conventional landscape of lawns, shade trees and benches.

The quarry itself, once the source of basalt for the roads of Shaughnessy Heights, is now the pride of the park—a landscape of wide lawns and flower beds enclosed by craggy walls of rough stone. In this pro-

tected shangri-la, against a background of vivid green grass, exotic plants like bananas, cannas and apricot-flowered abutilon cheat the climate late into fall. At centre stage, weeping beeches flank a magnificent swamp cypress which rises like a green pyramid from a swirl of neatly spaced annuals. A waterfall splashes down one rock face among crisply curling green ferns, its topmost reaches spanned by a curved Japanese bridge that lays fair claim to appearing in more wedding photographs than any other structure in Vancouver.

The high ground beyond the bridge is crowned by the faceted glass dome of the Bloedel Conservatory, a centennial project opened in 1969. Inside is yet another small world, this one a hothouse jungle of tropical plants and exotic birds.

One of the city's more remarkable gardens, and the

first full-scale classical Chinese garden to be built out-side China, is the Dr. Sun Yat-Sen Garden on Pender Street in the heart of Vancouver's historic Chinatown. Using only materials imported from China, right down to the pebbles inlaid in the courtyard paving, the garden embodies the Taoist principles of yin and yang—light balanced by shadow, rough texture by smooth. Enclosed within high white walls, the garden is essentially a large rectangle open to the sky where plants, rocks and water have been combined into an arrangement that mimics nature while yet appearing anything but natural. Branches are bent to cast just the right reflection in the jade-green water, "leak" windows in walls frame views as composed as landscape paintings, patterns of leaf and bark and flower are as carefully constructed as the mosaic of tile and pebble underfoot.

Dominating the garden is a small pagoda, or ting, on a rocky islet, its orange, turkscap roof like the flame on a great candle of molten wax. The pools of water that surround it, deliberately opaque to mirror their surroundings and the clouds that pass overhead, are dotted with waterlilies and spanned by small arches of stone.

Of all the city's public green spaces, one stands alone as a Vancouver icon. Stanley Park's downtown location and its immense size (1,000 acres) have allowed it to be all things to all people: a wilderness, a groomed garden, a place to swim, play tennis, picnic or simply watch the sun go down beyond the freighters at anchor in the harbour.

From the gardener's point of view, Stanley Park offers a variety of landscapes, reflecting on a grander scale some of those created by individuals in their own private domains. There are open meadows planted with deciduous trees of great individual beauty, wide lawns, lines of flowering fruit trees, broad herbaceous borders, a lagoon and a creek lined with weeping willows. There

is also an excellent rhododendron collection, where fallen trees have been left lying among the shrubs, their great discs of root upended to reveal a mosaic of earth and pebbles knotted together with ropes of gnarled wood. Nearby, rough-hewn planks surround the pitch-and-putt golf course, slotted at intervals into notches cut into massive, first-growth stumps.

From many vantage points in Stanley Park the indigenous forest of fir, cedar and hemlock competes with the towers of the West End to define the skyline. These are the extremes of Vancouver, the wilderness and the modern city, side by side. In gardens throughout the city, both public and private, a multitude of visions now occupies the middle ground. In the last quarter of a century, an educated, dedicated gardening community has emerged, inspired and encouraged by Vancouver's two botanical gardens, by local magazines wholly or partly devoted to gardening interests and by an increasing number of authoritative voices advising, suggesting and passing judgment on a wide variety of plants, styles and techniques for the benefit of the home gardener. The philosophy of the Canadian mosaic has invaded the garden, and in Vancouver, where a benign climate permits the indulgence of almost every gardening whim, determined individuals are taking advantage of their favoured location to enhance, challenge or defy the natural landscape in remarkable ways.

Nature decrees that a garden is always a work in progress, a volatile thing with an ephemeral past and an uncertain future. Despite the youth of this city, many carefully nurtured and beautiful gardens have already been lost—to development, to neglect, to an opposing vision. The aim of this book is to record a few of the best at a moment when Vancouver is in the midst of a gardening renaissance, to mark a particularly rich thread in the everchanging tapestry.

I have learned much, and am always learning, from other people's gardens, and the lesson I have learned most thoroughly is, never to say "I know" — there is so infinitely much to learn, and the conditions of different gardens vary so greatly, even when soil and situation appear to be alike and they are in the same district. —Gertrude Jekyll

THE GARDENS

WARMED IN WINTER by the temperate currents of the Pacific Ocean and cooled in summer by offshore breezes, Vancouver offers one of the most favourable climates in Canada for year-round gardening. Add fertile soil and a substantial annual rainfall, and you have the conditions that make it possible to cultivate virtually any plant the heart desires. A daring few, in the spirit of what one local trendsetter describes as "zonal denial," have even devoted their gardens to the cultivation of tropical species not normally tolerant of so northerly a home.

The gardens that follow are only a sample of the range of approaches to be found in this city. Here are glades that mimic the rainforest floor in the cool shadow of tall evergreens, formal green spaces where structure is the dominant element, exuberant medleys of cottage favourites in the English country style, sweeping perennial borders and meticulously plotted knot gardens. Whether influenced by the existing landscape, a passion for a particular species, the architecture of the house, the lay of the land, or an urge to push the boundaries, each gardener decides how much to acknowledge the great natural backdrop—the skyline of snow-capped mountains clad with the dark greens of cedar, hemlock, spruce and fir.

Their gardens vary in age from 50 years to less than five, some showing the results of decades of patience and care, others illustrating the quick rewards that determination and ingenuity can bring. In some, a single hand and eye has guided the composition; some are a collaboration between partners or friends, or between an owner and a professional landscaper or horticultural consultant; a few have been passed from one generation to another, the original design modified and embellished by younger gardeners open to a host of influences from around the world and blessed with a wide array of landscaping materials and plants to choose from.

Finally, these gardens have something to offer in all seasons of the year. An appreciation of shape as well as colour, a discriminating eye for the textures of green on green, grey on blue, an understanding of the movement of the sun and its effect on shadows, a knowledge of when and how plants unfurl, flower and decay—all these are reflected in the planning and planting that makes these gardens beautiful.

MARY STEWART'S GARDEN

"I'm mostly perennials, but I don't scorn annuals. I find some of them very useful."

MARY STEWART HAS BEEN TENDING the same piece of land in Kerrisdale for 50 years. When she and her husband moved into the half-timbered Tudor house, the three-quarter-acre property came with nothing more than a young white wisteria and the tall native cedars that still dominate the landscape.

Today, ribbons of wisteria wrap the house's southern facade. A green lawn flows gently between wide perennial borders, curving around the broad trunk of a single conical cedar in the middle distance and lapping up against the vertical wall of similar giants which might, with a slight effort of imagination, mark the edge of vast tracts of virgin rainforest. Sheltered by their bulk on one side and the height of the borders on the others, the garden seems remote from its neighbours, an illusion shattered only by the barking of a dog beyond the screen of foliage.

With such tall evergreens as a backdrop, trees within the garden appear in sharper contrast, and variations in the shapes and hues of their leaves—the silver feathers of a weeping, willow-leaf pear, the ruby red lockets of *Cercis* 'Forest Pansy', the polished leather of a magnolia—seem more pronounced. Many of these ornamental trees were among the first plantings in the garden, put in when the children were small and later enhanced by the shrubs and perennials that now surround them. The age of a purple smokebush (*Cotinus coggygria*) shows in the size of its gnarled old branches looping gracefully towards the patio. *Rhododendron* 'Pink Pearl' across the lawn, now 40 years old, is equally substantial.

Oldest of all in the garden are bearded irises. When Mary married, her father invited her to choose what she would like to take from his garden to her new home

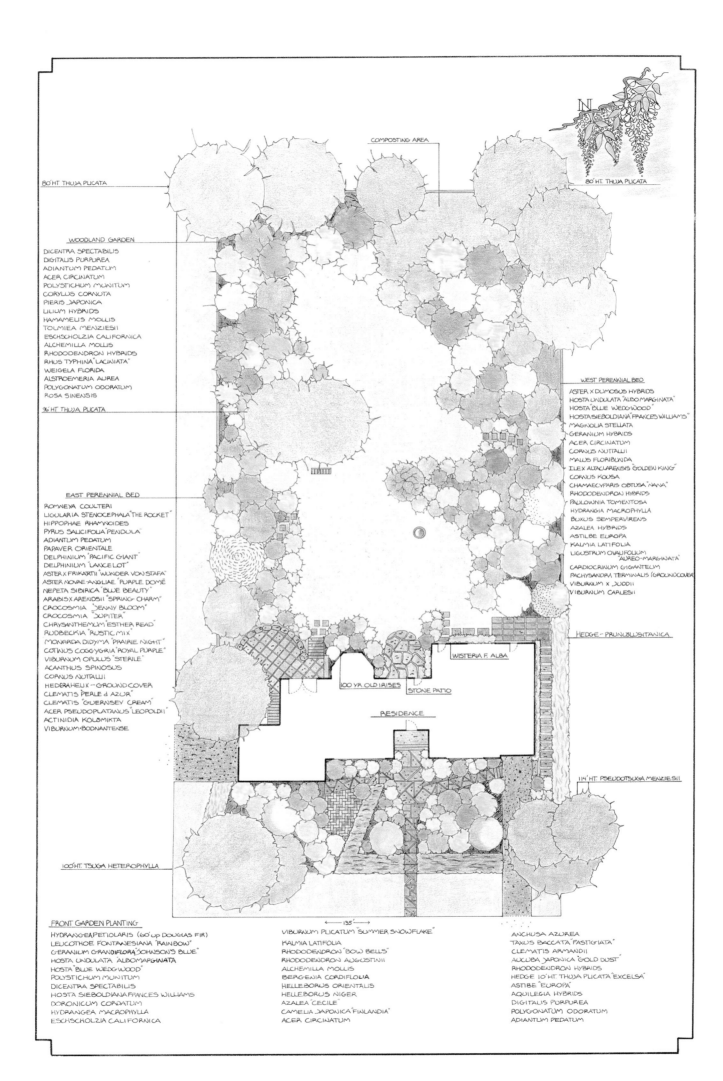

COMPOSTING AREA

80' HT. THUJA PLICATA

80' HT. THUJA PLICATA

N

WOODLAND GARDEN

DICENTRA SPECTABILIS
DIGITALIS PURPUREA
ADIANTUM PEDATUM
ACER CIRCINATUM
POLYSTICHUM MUNITUM
CORYLUS CORNUTA
PIERIS JAPONICA
LILIUM HYBRIDS
HAMAMELIS MOLLIS
TOLMIEA MENZIESII
ESCHSCHOLZIA CALIFORNICA
ALCHEMILLA MOLLIS
RHODODENDRON HYBRIDS
RHUS TYPHINA "LACINIATA"
WEIGELA FLORIDA
ALSTROEMERIA AUREA
POLYGONATUM ODORATUM
ROSA SINENSIS

36' HT. THUJA PLICATA

WEST PERENNIAL BED

ASTER X DUMOSUS HYBRIDS
HOSTA UNDULATA "ALBO MARGINATA"
HOSTA "BLUE WEDGWOOD"
HOSTA SIEBOLDIANA "FRANCES WILLIAMS"
MAGNOLIA STELLATA
GERANIUM HYBRIDS
ACER CIRCINATUM
CORNUS NUTTALLII
MALUS FLORIBUNDA
ILEX ALTACLARENSIS "GOLDEN KING"
CORNUS KOUSA
CHAMAECYPARIS OBTUSA "NANA"
RHODODENDRON HYBRIDS
PAULOWNIA TOMENTOSA
HYDRANGIA MACROPHYLLA
BUXUS SEMPERVIRENS
AZALEA HYBRIDS
ASTILBE EUROPA
KALMIA LATIFOLIA
LIGUSTRUM OVALIFOLIUM
   "AUREO-MARGINATA"
CARDIOCRINUM GIGANTEUM
PACHYSANDRA TERMINALIS (GROUNDCOVER)
VIBURNUM X JUDDII
VIBURNUM CARLESII

EAST PERENNIAL BED

ROMNEYA COULTERI
LIGULARIA STENOCEPHALA "THE ROCKET"
HIPPOPHAE RHAMNOIDES
PYRUS SALICIFOLIA "PENDULA"
ADIANTUM PEDATUM
PAPAVER ORIENTALE
DELPHINIUM "PACIFIC GIANT"
DELPHINIUM "LANCELOT"
ASTER X FRIKARTII "WUNDER VON STAFA"
ASTER NOVAE-ANGLIAE "PURPLE DOME"
NEPETA SIBIRICA "BLUE BEAUTY"
ARABIS X ARENDSII "SPRING CHARM"
CROCOSMIA "JENNY BLOOM"
CROCOSMIA "JUPITER"
CHRYSANTHEMUM "ESTHER READ"
RUDBECKIA "RUSTIC MIX"
MONARDA DIDYMA "PRAIRIE NIGHT"
COTINUS COGGYGRIA "ROYAL PURPLE"
VIBURNUM OPULUS "STERILE"
ACANTHUS SPINOSUS
CORNUS NUTTALLII
HEDERA HELIX – GROUND COVER
CLEMATIS "PERLE d AZUR"
CLEMATIS "GUERNSEY CREAM"
ACER PSEUDOPLATANUS "LEOPOLDII"
ACTINIDIA KOLOMIKTA
VIBURNUM·BODNANTENSE.

HEDGE - PRUNUS LUSITANICA

WISTERIA F. ALBA

100 YR. OLD IRISES

STONE PATIO

RESIDENCE

114' HT. PSEUDOTSUGA MENZIESII

100' HT. TSUGA HETEROPHYLLA

← 135' →

FRONT GARDEN PLANTING

HYDRANGEA PETIOLARIS (60' up DOUGLAS FIR)
LEUCOTHOE FONTANESIANA "RAINBOW"
GERANIUM GRANDIFLORA "JOHNSON'S BLUE"
HOSTA UNDULATA "ALBOMARGINATA"
HOSTA "BLUE WEDGWOOD"
POLYSTICHUM MUNITUM
DICENTRA SPECTABILIS
HOSTA SIEBOLDIANA FRANCES WILLIAMS
DORONICUM CORDATUM
HYDRANGEA MACROPHYLLA
ESCHSCHOLZIA CALIFORNICA

VIBURNUM PLICATUM "SUMMER SNOWFLAKE"
KALMIA LATIFOLIA
RHODODENDRON "BOW BELLS"
RHODODENDRON AUGUSTINII
ALCHEMILLA MOLLIS
BERGENIA CORDIFOLIA
HELLEBORUS ORIENTALIS
HELLEBORUS NIGER
AZALEA "CECILE"
CAMELIA JAPONICA "FINLANDIA"
ACER CIRCINATUM

ANCHUSA AZUREA
TAXUS BACCATA "FASTIGIATA"
CLEMATIS ARMANDII
AUCUBA JAPONICA "GOLD DUST"
RHODODENDRON HYBRIDS
HEDGE 10' HT. THUJA PLICATA "EXCELSA"
ASTILBE "EUROPA"
AQUILEGIA HYBRIDS
DIGITALIS PURPUREA
POLYGONATUM ODORATUM
ADIANTUM PEDATUM

"If I have to choose between plain and variegated, I always choose plain."

and she selected these, knowing them to be among his favourites too. They have now spent almost a hundred years with father and daughter, and in spite of the attractions of many plants that Mary has acquired since, she continues to believe that "the best time in the garden is iris time."

Other plants recall other friends. A group of *Cardiocrinum giganteum* under the magnolia were a gift from Gerald Straley, the late director of UBC's botanical garden. Their cream trumpets appear only every six years; hers have already bloomed twice. Another friend willed Mary some white and pink tree peonies she had admired, and to her delight "they moved beautifully."

A plant collector with an artist's eye for design, Mary fills her wide borders with a fascinating array of perennials, and a few "useful" annuals. Although there are the traditional mainstays like phlox, delphiniums and what Mary calls "an orchard mix" of lilies, there are also plants quite new to Vancouver gardens, such as a Matelija poppy (*Romneya coulteri),* or a gloriosa daisy called 'Irish Eyes' whose rayed golden petals surround a startling green centre. Here is a tuft of ornamental grass, pin-striped in crisp white and green, and over there a group of five tall *Cimicifuga,* their bristly white flowerheads curving like shepherd's crooks.

Many of these individual plants, although eye-catching in themselves, are yet part of a larger picture, grouped with others in matching hues. It may be just the golden eye of the Matelija poppy catching a reflection from the petals of 'Irish Eyes', or a pale pink balloon flower next to *Sidalcea* 'Loveliness' and the rosier pink of *Centranthus ruber,* or it may be the contrasting shapes of 'Lady Plymouth' and 'White Glory'—two very different but equally white pelargoniums in an urn. To Mary, "plants seem to have a right to a certain place."

Far down the garden, the lawn comes to an end in a cool, woodland area where ferns, foxgloves and bleeding hearts enjoy the shade under the towering cedars. Witch hazel blooms bring fragrance in early spring; vine maples and sumac close out the end of the year with flaming crimson and orange foliage. *Alstroemeria aurea* has run wild among the other plants in these beds, carrying yellow highlights all the way down the garden. While Mary likes white and a lot of blue for the broader strokes of colour, she concedes that she considers yellow very helpful for linking different areas.

This south-facing garden is by far the larger section of the property and in spite of the height of the surrounding trees, most of it is open to the summer sun. On the north side, the garden is smaller and shadier but just as densely planted—perhaps more so as it has no lawn to fill the middle ground, just a stone-flagged path where seeds of *Astrantia* 'Shaggy' have self-sown in the cracks. The path slips in from the broad grassy boulevard through a narrow gap in a tall, dark cedar hedge. Imposing shrubs crowd up to it on either side, their presence softened by flowers of gentle colours. The silver-green starbursts of 'Shaggy', blue mopheads of a hydrangea, and horizontal white flower clusters of a *Viburnum plicatum* have a cool, rainforest air quite different from the vitality of the perennial borders on the sunny side of the house. Willowy stems of *Thalictrum flavum* sway against the viburnum, their fern-like foliage as suffused with blue as the downy leaves of nearby *Rhododendron augustinii.* Hellebores and hostas continue the silver, white and green colour scheme at ground level, and a climbing hydrangea (*Hydrangea petiolaris*) carries it high into the branches of a Douglas fir.

Fifty years of Mary's care, informed by her formidable store of knowledge, has brought this garden to its present glory. "You learn to be patient," she muses. "Now my work is mostly pruning and cutting down." ❧

PAGE 32
Silver foliage of a willow-leafed pear (*Pyrus salicifolia pendula*) and artemisia contrasts with magenta flowers of Geranium 'Anne Folkard'.

PAGE 33
Alstroemeria aurea.

PAGE 35
White *Wisteria sinensis alba* garlands the south facade.

PAGE 37
Giant himalayan lily (*Cardiocrinum giganteum*) flowers only once every six years.

PAM FROST'S GARDEN

"The surrounding trees impose themselves on the landscape so much.
I wanted a garden that would fit in, not be at odds
with its surroundings."

WHEN PAM FROST took some graph paper and began to draw a plan of her new property, she was astonished at how long and narrow it was. It eventually required two pieces of graph paper tacked together to accurately represent its dimensions of 63 feet by 342 feet.

Now, 30 years later, you can still look from the back deck all the way to the western boundary of the double-depth garden in Kerrisdale, but your eye travels slowly, meandering along a river of green lawn and stopping frequently to inspect a burst of bright foliage or a drift of petals in the deep borders that create a subtle illusion of breadth.

The most prominent feature of these borders is a tall *Robinia pseudoacacia* 'Frisia', which occupies a "headland" in the middle distance, its lower branches drooping gracefully over the lawn as if seeking its own reflection in the pool of green. What Pam likes best about it is the way its golden leaves hold the light on dark days. Now easily obtainable, it was rare enough when Pam acquired it that she had to send to the famous Hillier's nursery in England to obtain a young sapling.

As it grew, its brilliant colour was so arresting that it became too much of a focal point in the garden. "Your eye went to it and stopped," Pam recalls. "I had to plant another further down to draw the eye on." The second robinia is now threatening to catch up to the first in height, much to Pam's dismay, as she likes the exaggerated perspective their juxtaposition lends to the view.

In midsummer, the sunshine colour of the robinia foliage is echoed by the leaves of a golden hop vine (*Humulus lupulus* 'Aureus') weaving in and out of the shrubs massed along the fence, and by a golden privet

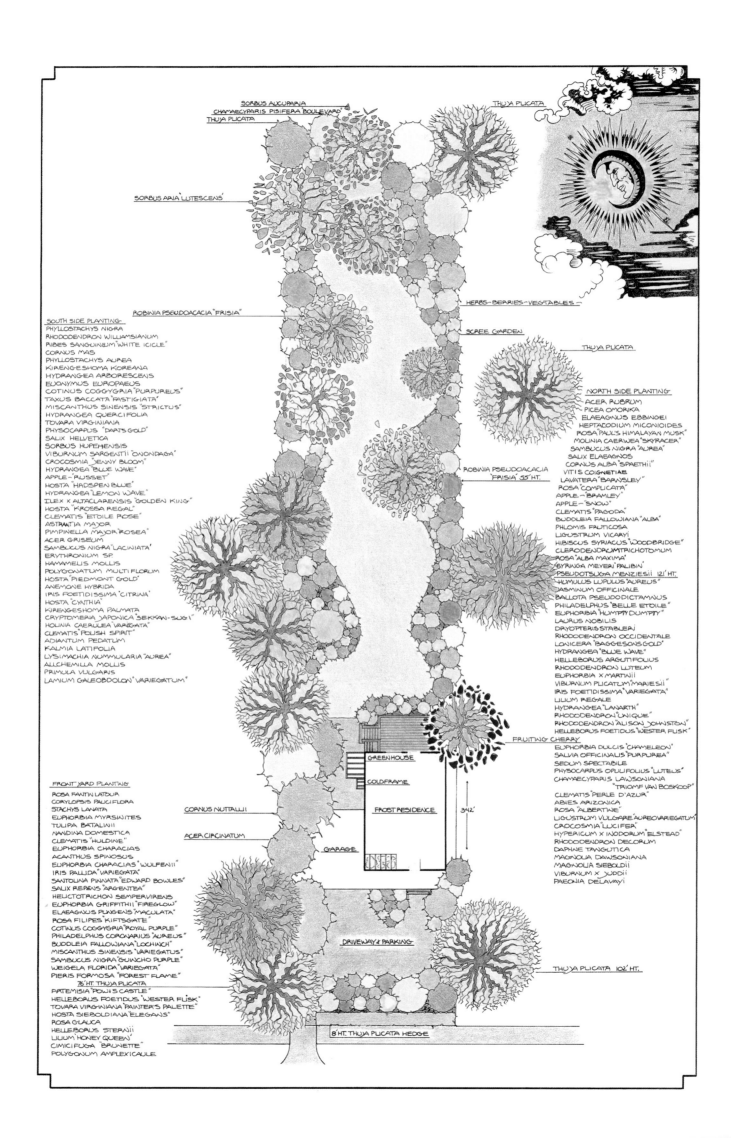

whose bushy silhouette is spiked with skewers of flame-coloured *Crocosmia* 'Lucifer'. When a western swallow-tail butterfy pauses here on its way to a nearby white buddleia, it adds a little dancing jewel of black and citrine to complete the harmony.

A confessed plant collector, Pam is also a skilled amateur artist and her garden reflects an understanding of composition and colour theory as much as it displays the results of her forays in search of the unusual and intriguing. The long borders, one of which is wet and one dry, are divided by colour scheme, too, into a "hot" border and a "cool" one. In the hot border, the dark bronze foliage of *Dahlia* 'Bishop of Llandaff' blends with the claret leaves of a smokebush, the storm-cloud tones of heucheras, and the little purple grape-like balls of an *Anemonopsis*. Pushing through the smokebush leaves are bells of *Nectaroscordum siculum*, a tall member of the onion family with petals of softest lavender pink streaked with plum. In the same bed, a hydrangea relative, *Deinanthe caerulea*, wears little drooping teardrops of amethyst. Spaced along the entire length are clumps of *Sedum spectabile* and ground-hugging patches of *Ajuga* 'Metallica crispa' to tie the disparate elements together. In this rich setting of so many shades of purple and burnished brown, the blood-red flowers of the dahlia shine like jewels on velvet.

At the back of the border, clematis in matching hues adorn the fence—ruby red 'Etoile Rouge' and white 'Huldine', striped in soft lilac. "My mother told me to grow 'Huldine' where you can look up at it," says Pam, "because the stripes are only on the underside." Her mother has been a strong influence on the garden, both on visits from her home in England and also through the copious letters she has written after each return, suggesting plant choices or combinations. Pam's daughter, Katherine, brings yet another generation's perspective to the garden and has claimed a small area at the far end for her own ideas. "It is interesting," Pam comments inscrutably, "to see how it's developing."

The border that stretches along the north side of the property is the one that gets the most sun. The dryness of the soil here has given Pam the opportunity to experiment with a scree garden, where tiny cushions of dianthus and geranium and clumps of shrubby penstemon and hebe dot a patch of gravel. This is also the side dominated by cool colours: white hydrangeas, jasmine and roses, pale yellow whorls of *Phlomis russeliana*, tiny soft lime trumpets of *Nicotiana langsdorffii* and of course many plants with cool green or grey foliage. Sharp contrasts here and there and an occasional splash of brighter colour add vitality to the composition. The lime of the nicotiana is echoed by a rim around the flowers of an *Alstroemeria psittacina*, but the spokes of each wheel-like bloom are a vivid scarlet, and this colour appears again when the late-flowering *Clematis texensis* 'Gravetye Beauty' blooms. Farther along, the jagged foliage and frosty blue stems of a cardoon are screened by a purple orach whose leaves are almost black.

Behind a nearby row of raspberries, a rambling rose, 'Paul's Himalayan Musk', encloses the end of the garden, climbing high into the surrounding foliage. In summer its clusters of pale pink flowers fill the air with their perfume.

Close to the house, many of the plants are fragrant, among them magnolias, daphne and *Viburnum × juddii* which produces tiny pale pink flowers in large spherical clusters. Tucked to one side is a greenhouse and a cold frame. "I raise a lot of plants from seed," Pam says. "When I read a description like 'comes from the high Himalayas', it sounds so enticing." She reads a great deal, counting authors like Christopher Lloyd, Beth Chatto and Michael Pollan among her influences, and particularly enjoys "books I disagree with."

By contrast with the huge back garden, the area in front of the house is small, and mostly paved to provide access for cars; around the perimeter, there is nevertheless room for a surprising number of interesting plants. Here, foliage colours play a large part, from the many silvery blue shades of *Rosa glauca, Buddleia* 'Lochinch', *Santolina* and *Artemisia* 'Powis Castle' to the deep mahogany of a smokebush and a black elder. In between are the green and cream stripes of variegated iris and weigela, and the tall blades of maiden grass (*Miscanthus sinensis*). On the shallow steps that lead to the front door a collection of containers brimming with flowers and foliage changes with the changing seasons.

A cedar hedge, with two tall conifers as bookends, screens the property from the sidewalk. From the street an alert observer looking skyward may notice 'Kiftsgate', a giant of a rose scaling one of the trees. Easily visible above the hedge, it spills trusses of white flowers over its host in summer and sprinkles it with festive red berries in winter. Only this rose and a glimpse of the garden from the driveway entrance give the curious passerby a hint of the tranquil garden of many treasures hidden within. ᴄ፥

PAGE 38
Contrasting leaf shapes of
*Aucuba japonica, Alchemilla
mollis, Leucothoe fontan-
esiana* and *Polystichum
munitum.*

PAGE 39
Airy flowers of *Astrantia
major.*

PAGE 41
Hosta fortunei 'Francee'
envelops a tree trunk.

PAGE 43
Robinia pseudoacacia 'Frisia'
dominates the long back
garden.

DIANA COOPER'S GARDEN

"I work on the diagonal – try to make everything into a vista.
I like a lot of curves, and concentrate on leaves. "

DIANA COOPER'S HOUSE IS PART of a late 1920s development laid out by a builder whose subdivision plan called for alternating Georgian and Tudor-style houses along every street. Hers is one of the Tudor designs, painted in the traditional white with grey and black trim. In keeping with the architecture, the garden also borrows from the English style with wide mixed borders and leafy paths.

Along the busy street frontage runs a tall, dense cedar hedge, broken only by a narrow driveway overhung with wisteria. In the shade created by the height of the hedge and a tall deodar cedar on the northwest corner, rhododendrons flourish in an underplanting of cool hosta leaves and trails of ivy. Most of the plants here are easy-care shrubs with some spring bulbs interspersed for early colour. The noise of traffic from the road outside, although muted, is insistent enough to discourage lingering on this side of the house, though its dapple of sunlight and shadow, echoed in the rich greens and purples of contrasting foliage, attracts the other senses. When Diana works here, she usually wears headphones and listens to opera. During tragic arias, she gardens through her tears.

Access around the house is under a lych gate, past a border of blue-leaved plants and pale-flowered shade lovers like white foxgloves and *Epimedium* 'White Queen', then finally through another hefty gate draped with *Clematis* 'Blue Ravine'. In the long back garden on the other side, a curving sweep of lawn spreads between broad beds of perennials and shrubs. "The lawn is really important in this garden," says Diana, "because it defines the beds."

The property has been in her family since 1928 when her grandmother bought it and soon after had it profes-

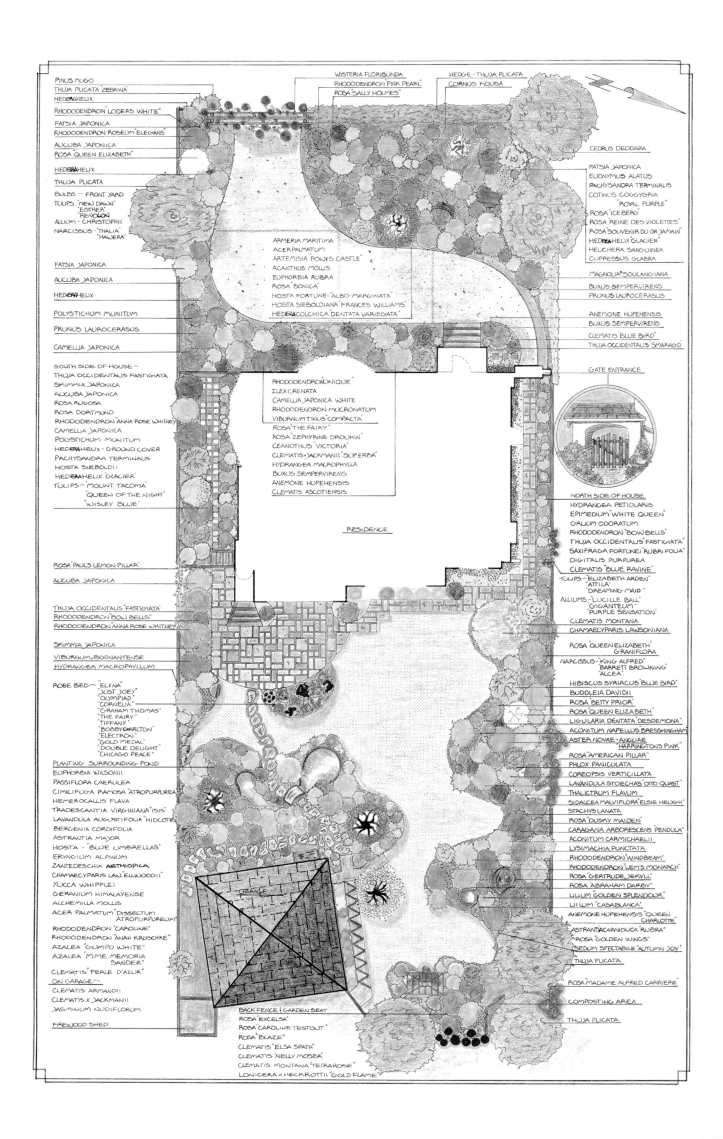

PINUS MUGO
THUJA PLICATA "ZEBRINA"
HEDERA HELIX
RHODODENDRON "LODERS WHITE"
FATSIA JAPONICA
RHODODENDRON ROSEUM ELEGANS
AUCUBA JAPONICA
ROSA "QUEEN ELIZABETH"

HEDERA HELIX
THUJA PLICATA
BULBS - FRONT YARD
TULIPS "NEW DAWN"
        "ESTHER"
        "RENOWN"
ALLIUM - CHRISTOPHII
NARCISSUS "THALIA"
         "HAWERA"

FATSIA JAPONICA
AUCUBA JAPONICA
HEDERA HELIX
POLYSTICHUM MUNITUM
PRUNUS LAUROCERASUS
CAMELLIA JAPONICA

SOUTH SIDE OF HOUSE ~
THUJA OCCIDENTALIS FASTIGIATA
SKIMMIA JAPONICA
AUCUBA JAPONICA
ROSA RUGOSA
ROSA DORTMUND
RHODODENDRON "ANNA ROSE WHITNEY"
CAMELLIA JAPONICA
POLYSTICHUM MUNITUM
HEDERA HELIX - GROUND COVER
PACHYSANDRA TERMINALIS
HOSTA SIEBOLDII
HEDERA HELIX "GLACIER"
TULIPS - "MOUNT TACOMA"
        "QUEEN OF THE NIGHT"
        "WISLEY BLUE"

ROSA "PAULS LEMON PILLAR"

AUCUBA JAPONICA

THUJA OCCIDENTALIS "FASTIGIATA"
RHODODENDRON "BOW BELLS"
RHODODENDRON "ANNA ROSE WHITNEY"

SKIMMIA JAPONICA
VIBURNUM "BODNANTENSE"
HYDRANGEA MACROPHYLLUM

ROSE BED ~ "ELINA"
           "JUST JOEY"
           "OLYMPIAD"
           "CORNELIA"
           "GRAHAM THOMAS"
           "THE FAIRY"
           "TIFFANY"
           "BOBBY CHARLTON"
           "ELECTRON"
           "GOLD MEDAL"
           "DOUBLE DELIGHT"
           "CHICAGO PEACE"

PLANTING SURROUNDING POND
EUPHORBIA WILSONII
PASSIFLORA CAERULEA
CIMICIFUGA RAMOSA "ATROPURPUREA"
HEMEROCALLIS FLAVA
TRADESCANTIA VIRGINIANA "ISIS"
LAVANDULA AUGUSTIFOLIA "HIDCOTE"
BERGENIA CORDIFOLIA
ASTRANTIA MAJOR
HOSTA - "BLUE UMBRELLAS"
ERYNGIUM ALPINUM
ZANTEDESCHIA AETHIOPICA
CHAMAECYPARIS LAW. "ELLWOODII"
YUCCA WHIPPLEI
GERANIUM HIMALAYENSE
ALCHEMILLA MOLLIS
ACER PALMATUM "DISSECTUM
             ATROPURPUREUM"
RHODODENDRON "CAROLINE"
RHODODENDRON "ANAH KRUSCHKE"
AZALEA "GUMPO WHITE"
AZALEA "MME. MEMORIA
        SANDER"
CLEMATIS "PERLE D'AZUR"
ON GARAGE ~
CLEMATIS ARMANDII
CLEMATIS X JACKMANII
JASMINUM NUDIFLORUM

FIREWOOD SHED

ARMERIA MARITIMA
ACER PALMATUM
ARTEMISIA "POWIS CASTLE"
ACANTHUS MOLLIS
EUPHORBIA RUBRA
ROSA "BONICA"
HOSTA FORTUNEI "ALBO-MARGINATA"
HOSTA SIEBOLDIANA "FRANCES WILLIAMS"
HEDERA COLCHICA "DENTATA VARIEGATA"

RHODODENDRON "UNIQUE"
ILEX CRENATA
CAMELLIA JAPONICA WHITE
RHODODENDRON MUCRONATUM
VIBURNUM TINUS "COMPACTA"
ROSA "THE FAIRY"
ROSA "ZEPHYRINE DROUHIN"
CEANOTHUS "VICTORIA"
CLEMATIS "JACKMANII SUPERBA"
HYDRANGEA MACROPHYLLA
BUXUS SEMPERVIRENS
ANEMONE HUPEHENSIS
CLEMATIS ASCOTIENSIS

RESIDENCE

WISTERIA FLORIBUNDA
RHODODENDRON "PINK PEARL"
ROSA "SALLY HOLMES"

HEDGE - THUJA PLICATA
CORNUS KOUSA

CEDRUS DEODARA

FATSIA JAPONICA
EUONYMUS ALATUS
PACHYSANDRA TERMINALIS
COTINUS COGGYGRIA
         "ROYAL PURPLE"
ROSA "ICEBERG"
ROSA "REINE DES VIOLETTES"
ROSA "SOUVENIR DU DR JAMAIN"
HEDERA HELIX "GLACIER"
HEUCHERA SANGUINEA
CUPRESSUS GLABRA

MAGNOLIA "SOULANGIANA"
BUXUS SEMPERVIRENS
PRUNUS LAUROCERASUS

ANEMONE HUPEHENSIS
BUXUS SEMPERVIRENS
CLEMATIS "BLUE BIRD"
THUJA OCCIDENTALIS "SMARAGD"

GATE ENTRANCE

NORTH SIDE OF HOUSE
HYDRANGEA PETIOLARIS
EPIMEDIUM "WHITE QUEEN"
GALIUM ODORATUM
RHODODENDRON "BOW BELLS"
THUJA OCCIDENTALIS "FASTIGIATA"
SAXIFRAGA FORTUNEI "RUBRIFOLIA"
DIGITALIS PURPUREA
CLEMATIS "BLUE RAVINE"
TULIPS "ELIZABETH ARDEN"
       "ATTILA"
       "DREAMING MAID"
ALLIUMS - "LUCILLE BALL"
          "GIGANTEUM"
          "PURPLE SENSATION"
CLEMATIS MONTANA
CHAMAECYPARIS LAWSONIANA

ROSA "QUEEN ELIZABETH"
     GRANIFLORA
NARCISSUS - "KING ALFRED"
            "BARRETT BROWNING"
            "ALCEA"
HIBISCUS SYRIACUS "BLUE BIRD"
BUDDLEIA DAVIDII
ROSA "BETTY PRIOR"
ROSA "QUEEN ELIZABETH"
LIGULARIA DENTATA "DESDEMONA"
ACONITUM NAPELLUS "BRESSHINGHAM"
ASTER NOVAE - ANGLIAE
      "HARRINGTONS PINK"
ROSA "AMERICAN PILLAR"
PHLOX PANICULATA
COREOPSIS VERTICILLATA
LAVANDULA STOECHAS "OTTO QUAST"
THALICTRUM FLAVUM
SIDALCEA MALVIFLORA "ELSIE HEUGH"
STACHYS LANATA
ROSA "DUSKY MAIDEN"
CARAGANA ARBORESCENS "PENDULA"
ACONITUM CARMICHAELII
LYSIMACHIA PUNCTATA
RHODODENDRON "WINDBEAM"
RHODODENDRON "LEMS MONARCH"
ROSA "GERTRUDE JEKYLL"
ROSA "ABRAHAM DARBY"
LILIUM "GOLDEN SPLENDOUR"
LILIUM "CASABLANCA"
ANEMONE HUPEHENSIS "QUEEN
         CHARLOTTE"
ASTRANTIA CARNIOLICA "RUBRA"
ROSA "GOLDEN WINGS"
SEDUM SPECTABILE "AUTUMN JOY"
THUJA PLICATA

ROSA "MADAME ALFRED CARRIERE"

COMPOSTING AREA

THUJA PLICATA

GARAGE

BACK FENCE & GARDEN SEAT
ROSA "EXCELSA"
ROSA "CAROLINE TESTOUT"
ROSA "BLAZE"
CLEMATIS "ELSA SPATH"
CLEMATIS "NELLY MOSER"
CLEMATIS MONTANA "TETRAROSE"
LONICERA X HECKROTTII "GOLD FLAME"

sionally landscaped. The plan has remained basically the same since, except for changes required by the growth of certain trees and shrubs to maturity. Two small ponds had to be moved forward because the rhododendron behind them had grown so large it overwhelmed them. Fifteen forest trees at the back of the lot have now been reduced to three tall cedars. "They were planted too close together," recalls Diana. "Everything was dead for about 15 feet up."

Within the original layout, however, she has made many changes. Paths wind among the beds, changing materials as they go so that circular pavers set into grass give way to a ribbon of smooth concrete over a tiny bridge, then rough irregular slabs and finally neat brick squares. The bridge separates the redesigned pond into two pools and here too the pattern changes. On one side a waterfall creates constant movement and flickering light; on the other the water is still and reflective, a mirror for the small stone hedgehog that gazes into its depths.

At strategic points a striking plant or a bench is carefully set to catch the eye, although Diana herself rarely finds an opportunity to sit when she is in her garden. If she does, it might be at a small table near the house within a half-moon of fragrant roses underplanted with annuals like begonias and heliotrope. This is also a cutting garden because Diana likes "bowls and bowls of roses in the house." Her favourite rose, 'Paul's Lemon Pillar', which droops huge fragrant creamy flowers along the south fence, dates from the original planting. It shares its position with two rampant clematis—pure white 'Madame Le Coultre' and blue 'Ramona'.

Combining plants successfully is one of Diana's signatures. Yellow daylilies surround a *Zantedeschia ethiopica*, colour-matched to its pollen-coated central style; the white stripes of a variegated hosta harmonize with the white bells of a bleeding heart; deeply cut silver leaves of *Artemisia* 'Powis Castle' trace a similar delicate pattern to purple ones of a Japanese maple, while between them *Centranthus ruber* makes the colour transition, its flowers a soft echo of the maple, its leaves a darker, coarser version of the artemisia.

Another feature of the garden is its element of surprise, born out of the owner's sense of humour. Walk down the narrow, shrub-filled passage along the south side of the house and you will unexpectedly come face to face with your own image. A tall mirror bars the way, so discreetly framed and so cleverly angled that you are not aware of it until you are a footstep from its surface. The pink rhododendron you imagine you are approaching is in fact behind you. An obelisk of dove-grey wood that supports a cascade of clematis and passionflower vine is the centrepiece of this little corridor, giving it height but not bulk. It also serves to screen Diana's view from her study of her neighbour's kitchen window.

On the other side of the garden under an arbour hung with an 'American Pillar' rose, a shelf attached to the fence holds a small terracotta pot shaped like a human head. From its cranium sprouts a punk tuft of blue oat grass. Another pot on the back porch contains a miniature forest, which close inspection reveals to be a clump of purple basil seedlings. Even in the planting combinations Diana cannot resist a quixotic touch. Among the many plants growing up and through their companions, one pairing—a small-leafed azalea springing above a young Japanese maple—has just the look of a sunhat on a mass of wispy hair. And surely there's a metaphor in the siting of *Hosta* 'Blue Umbrella' beside the little waterfall.

In the back lane, more roses and clematis overhang the fence. Two white wooden planters nailed to the fence hold a riot of orange and yellow nasturtiums, and beans and arugula grow in a half-barrel. This is Diana's vegetable garden: the nasturtium petals are for sandwiches, the arugula for salads, and as for the beans . . . "they're the only vegetable I can grow," she admits.

PAGE 44
Ferns, hostas and ivies fill a
cool, north-facing passageway.

PAGE 45
Hydrangea macrophylla.

PAGE 47
Pale yellow rose 'Elina' and a
blue hydrangea beside a path
into the back garden.

PAGE 48–49
Contrasting foliage of
Heuchera 'Palace Purple',
Pulmonaria officinalis, hostas
and a variegated ivy (*Hedera
colchica* 'Dentata Variegata')
surround a bird bath.

Although Diana spends her spare daylight hours
working among the plants, she has added lighting to the
garden so that she can enjoy it after dark from the com-
fort of the sunroom she has added to the back of the
house. Here she sits and contemplates her handiwork,
listening to the classical music that is her other source
of pleasure and relaxation. ❧

SHIRLEY HEBENTON'S GARDEN

"I like to know plants — know their names, understand their habits. Admiration is not enough."

IN WINTER IT IS A STUDY IN greys and greens. The grey trunks of a pair of weeping beeches flank each end of the front fence, their smooth undulating bark looking so curiously like elephant hide. Beneath their dangling branches, the silver-grey house crouches among dark rhododendrons and the green of a luxuriant laurel hedge. A pool of emerald moss laps the edges of the stone path to the black-painted door which is guarded by a pair of clipped box in grey planters.

There are no windows that face the front. From inside the house, diamond-paned windows look out at the back garden, past a small patio overhung with grapevines and over a wide expanse of lawn. Around its margin, low walls of grey stone divide the terrain into levels, ending where tall conifers close off the farther view. In winter, shafts of thin sunlight filter through these trees, highlighting the fretwork of branches on a quartet of Japanese maples around a tiny pond. With the coming of spring, young grape leaves on the pergola sheltering the patio add a fresh note of green to the foreground, while, back at the pond, the maples are unfurling feathers of reddish bronze. On the bank behind them, rhododendrons are in bud, looming among the rugged trunks of the conifers, their bright flowers slowly opening like lights going on at the beginning of a performance.

It is this kind of subtle effect that most pleases Shirley Hebenton. For 18 years she has been weaving patterns of colour and texture through her shady half-acre in upper Shaughnessy, a stone's throw (and a world) away from busy Granville Street. The 1922 bungalow, designed by architect James A. Benzie for his mother, had already been modified by an attic addition when the Hebentons bought it, and while the new part

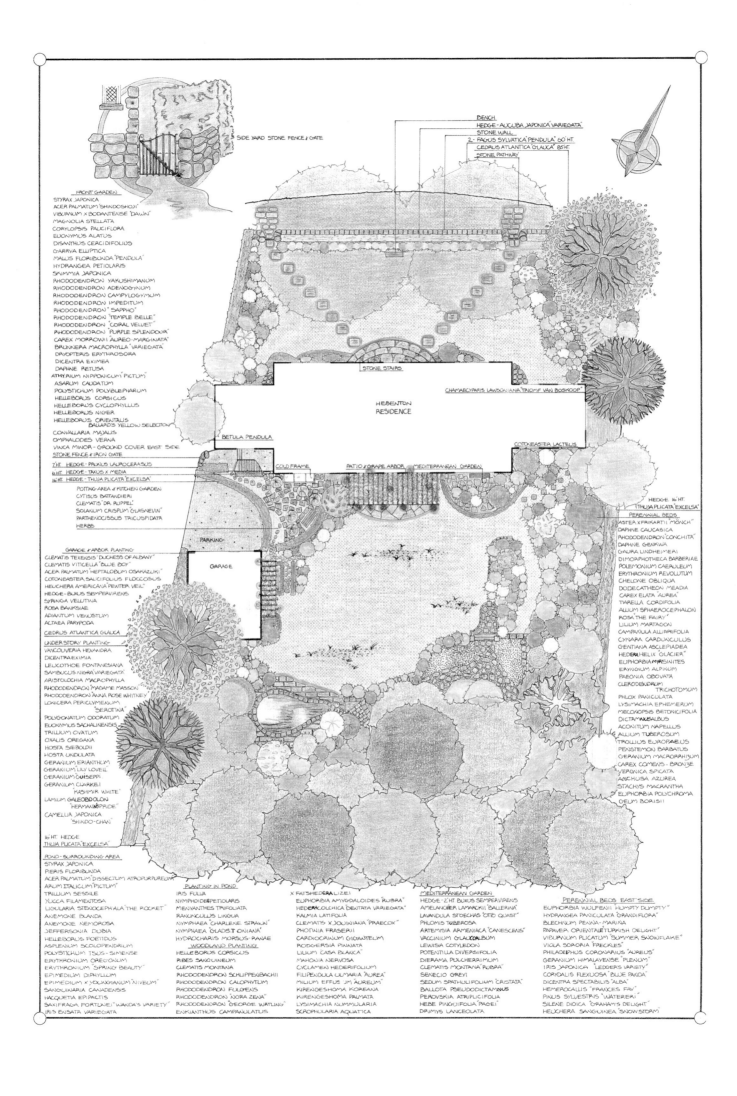

SIDE YARD STONE FENCE & GATE

BENCH
HEDGE - AUCUBA JAPONICA 'VARIEGATA'
STONE WALL
2 - FAGUS SYLVATICA 'PENDULA' 60' HT.
CEDRUS ATLANTICA 'GLAUCA' 85'HT.
STONE PATHWAY

STONE STAIRS

HEBENTON RESIDENCE

CHAMAECYPARIS LAWSONIANA 'TRIOMF VAN BOSKOOP'

BETULA PENDULA

COTONEASTER LACTEUS

COLD FRAME   PATIO / GRAPE ARBOR   MEDITERRANEAN GARDEN

HEDGE - 16' HT. 'THUJA PLICATA EXCELSA'

PARKING

GARAGE

FRONT GARDEN
STYRAX JAPONICA
ACER PALMATUM 'SHINDOSHOJI'
VIBURNUM X BODANTENSE 'DAWN'
MAGNOLIA STELLATA
CORYLOPSIS PALCIFLORA
EUONYMUS ALATUS
DISANTHUS CERCIDIFOLIUS
GARRYA ELLIPTICA
MALUS FLORIBUNDA 'PENDULA'
HYDRANGEA PETIOLARIS
SKIMMIA JAPONICA
RHODODENDRON YAKUSHIMANUM
RHODODENDRON ADENOGYNUM
RHODODENDRON CAMPYLOGYNUM
RHODODENDRON IMPEDITUM
RHODODENDRON 'SAPPHO'
RHODODENDRON 'TEMPLE BELLE'
RHODODENDRON 'CORAL VELVET'
RHODODENDRON 'PURPLE SPLENDOUR'
CAREX MORROWII 'AUREO-MARGINATA'
BRUNNERA MACROPHYLLA 'VARIEGATA'
DRYOPTERIS ERYTHROSORA
DICENTRA EXIMEA
DAPHNE RETUSA
ATHYRIUM NIPPONICUM 'PICTUM'
ASARUM CAUDATUM
POLYSTICHUM POLYBLEPHARUM
HELLEBORUS CORSICUS
HELLEBORUS CYCLOPHYLLUS
HELLEBORUS NIGER
HELLEBORUS ORIENTALIS 'BALLARD'S YELLOW SELECTION'
CONVALLARIA MAJALIS
OMPHALODES VERNA
VINCA MINOR - GROUND COVER EAST SIDE
STONE FENCE & IRON GATE

7' HT. HEDGE - PRUNUS LAUROCERASUS
6' HT. HEDGE - TAXUS X MEDIA
16' HT. HEDGE - THUJA PLICATA 'EXCELSA'

POTTING AREA & KITCHEN GARDEN
CYTISUS BATTANDIERI
CLEMATIS 'DR. RUPPEL'
SOLANUM CRISPUM 'GLASNEVIN'
PARTHENOCISSUS TRICUSPIDATA
HERBS

GARAGE & ARBOR PLANTING
CLEMATIS TEXENSIS 'DUCHESS OF ALBANY'
CLEMATIS VITICELLA 'BLUE BOY'
ACER PALMATUM 'HEPTALOBUM OSAKAZUKI'
COTONEASTER SALICIFOLIUS FLOCCOSUS
HEUCHERA AMERICANA 'PEWTER VEIL'
HEDGE - BUXUS SEMPERVIRENS
SYRINGA VELUTINA
ROSA BANKSIAE
ADIANTUM VENUSTUM
ACTAEA PARYPODA
CEDRUS ATLANTICA GLAUCA

UNDER STORY PLANTING
VANCOUVERIA HEXANDRA
DICENTRA EXIMIA
LEUCOTHOE FONTANESIANA
SAMBUCUS NIGRA 'VARIEGATA'
ARISTOLOCHIA MACROPHYLLA
RHODODENDRON 'MADAME MASSON'
RHODODENDRON 'ANNA ROSE WHITNEY'
LONICERA PERICLYMENUM 'SEROTINA'
POLYGONATUM ODORATUM
EUONYMUS SACHALINENSIS
TRILLIUM OVATUM
OXALIS OREGANA
HOSTA SIEBOLDII
HOSTA UNDULATA
GERANIUM ERIANTHUM
GERANIUM 'LILY LOVELL'
GERANIUM 'GUISEPPI'
GERANIUM CLARKEI 'KASHMIR WHITE'
LAMIUM GALEOBDOLON 'HERMAN'S PRIDE'
CAMELLIA JAPONICA 'SHINDO-CHAN'

16' HT. HEDGE
THUJA PLICATA 'EXCELSA'

POND - SURROUNDING AREA
STYRAX JAPONICA
PIERIS FLORIBUNDA
ACER PALMATUM 'DISSECTUM ATROPURPUREUM'
ARUM ITALICUM 'PICTUM'
TRILLIUM SESSILE
YUCCA FILAMENTOSA
LIGULARIA STENOCEPHALA 'THE ROCKET'
ANEMONE BLANDA
ANEMONE NEMOROSA
JEFFERSONIA DUBIA
HELLEBORUS FOETIDUS
ASPLENIUM SCOLOPENDRIUM
POLYSTICHUM TSUS-SIMENSE
ERYTHRONIUM OREGONUM
ERYTHRONIUM 'SPRING BEAUTY'
EPIMEDIUM DIPHYLLUM
EPIMEDIUM X YOUNGIANUM 'NIVEUM'
SANGUINARIA CANADENSIS
HACQUETIA EPIPACTIS
SAXIFRAGA FORTUNEI 'WANDA'S VARIETY'
IRIS ENSATA 'VARIEGATA'

PLANTING IN POND
IRIS FULVA
NYMPHOIDES PELTOLARIS
MENYANTHES TRIFOLIATA
RANUNCULUS LINGUA
NYMPHAEA 'CHARLENE STRAWN'
NYMPHAEA 'GLADSTONIANA'
HYDROCHARIS MORSUS-RANAE

WOODLAND PLANTING
HELLEBORUS CORSICUS
RIBES SANGUINEUM
CLEMATIS MONTANA
RHODODENDRON SCHLIPPENBACHII
RHODODENDRON CALOPHYTUM
RHODODENDRON FULGENS
RHODODENDRON 'NORA ZENA'
RHODODENDRON 'GEORGE WATLING'
ENKIANTHUS CAMPANULATUS

X FATSHEDERA LIZEI
EUPHORBIA AMYGDALOIDES 'RUBRA'
HEDERA COLCHICA 'DENTATA VARIEGATA'
KALMIA LATIFOLIA
CLEMATIS X JOUINIANA 'PRAECOX'
PHOTINIA FRASERII
CARDIOCRINUM GIGANTEUM
RODGERSIA PINNATA
LILIUM 'CASA BLANCA'
MAHONIA NERVOSA
CYCLAMEN HEDERIFOLIUM
FILIPENDULA ULMARIA 'AUREA'
MILIUM EFFUS JM 'AUREUM'
KIRENGESHOMA KOREANA
KIRENGESHOMA PALMATA
LYSIMACHIA NUMMULARIA
SCROPHULARIA AQUATICA

MEDITERRANEAN GARDEN
HEDGE - 2' HT BUXUS SEMPERVIRENS
AMELANCHIER LAMARCKII 'BALLERINA'
LAVANDULA STOECHAS 'OTTO QUAST'
PHLOMIS TUBEROSA
ARTEMISIA ARMENIACA 'CANESCENS'
VACCINIUM GLAUCOALBUM
LEWISIA COTYLEDON
POTENTILLA DIVERSIFOLIA
DIERAMA PULCHERRIMUM
CLEMATIS MONTANA 'RUBRA'
SENECIO GREYI
SEDUM SPATHULIFOLIUM 'CRISTATA'
BALLOTA PSEUDODICTAMNUS
PEROVSKIA ATRIPLICIFOLIA
HEBE PINGUIFOLIA 'PAGEI'
DRIMYS LANCEOLATA

PERENNIAL BEDS
ASTER X FRIKARTII 'MONCH'
DAPHNE CAUCASICA
RHODODENDRON 'CONCHITA'
DAPHNE GENKWA
GAURA LINDHEIMERI
DIMORPHOTHECA BARBERIAE
POLEMONIUM CAERULEUM
ERYTHRONIUM REVOLUTUM
CHELONE OBLIQUA
DODECATHEON MEADIA
CAREX ELATA 'AUREA'
TIARELLA CORDIFOLIA
ALLIUM SPHAEROCEPHALON
ROSA 'THE FAIRY'
LILIUM MARTAGON
CAMPANULA ALLIARIIFOLIA
CYNARA CARDUNCULUS
GENTIANA ASCLEPIADEA
HEDERA HELIX 'GLACIER'
EUPHORBIA MYRSINITES
ERYNGIUM ALPINUM
PAEONIA OBOVATA
CLERODENDRUM TRICHOTOMUM
PHLOX PANICULATA
LYSIMACHIA EPHEMERUM
MECONOPSIS BETONICIFOLIA
DICTAMNUS ALBUS
ACONITUM NAPELLUS
ALLIUM TUBEROSUM
TROLLIUS EUROPAEUS
PENSTEMON BARBATUS
GERANIUM MACRORRHIZUM
CAREX COMANS - BRONZE
VERONICA SPICATA
ANCHUSA AZUREA
STACHYS MACRANTHA
EUPHORBIA POLYCHROMA
GEUM BORISII

PERENNIAL BEDS EAST SIDE
EUPHORBIA WULFENII 'HUMPTY DUMPTY'
HYDRANGEA PANICULATA 'GRANDIFLORA'
BLECHNUM PENNA-MARINA
PAPAVER ORIENTALE 'TURKISH DELIGHT'
VIBURNUM PLICATUM 'SUMMER SNOWFLAKE'
VIOLA SORORIA 'FRECKLES'
PHILADELPHUS CORONARIUS 'AUREUS'
GERANIUM HIMALAYENSE 'PLENUM'
IRIS JAPONICA 'LEDGERS VARIETY'
CORYDALIS FLEXUOSA 'BLUE PANDA'
DICENTRA SPECTABILIS 'ALBA'
HEMEROCALLIS 'FRANCES FAY'
PINUS SYLVESTRIS 'WATERERI'
SILENE DIOICA 'GRAHAM'S DELIGHT'
HEUCHERA SANGUINEA 'SNOWSTORM'

blends imperceptibly into the old, Shirley regrets the loss of the original thatched roof visible in an early photograph. Also in the photograph is a young evergreen, identifiable as the substantial Atlas cedar which now competes with the beeches in the front garden. Little else occupied either this area or the broader sweep behind the house until Shirley began to fill in the blank canvas.

An active volunteer at nearby VanDusen Botanical Garden, Shirley has benefited from the friendship and advice of the garden's recently retired curator, Roy Forster. One of his gifts, a tiny rhododendron, now spreads an impressive 15 by 12 feet across the centre of the back boundary. Rhododendrons and the huge firs and cedars are the backbone of the garden, maintaining the illusion of a surrounding wilderness.

With her botanical connections, it's not surprising to find Shirley Hebenton so knowledgeable about her plants: their Latin names, their habits, what kind of soil

or how much shade they like. These facts are important to her and a horticultural dictionary is always by her back door. "I want a certain control over them," she says, at the same time conceding that "if a plant finds a good home by itself, I let it be." Around the margin of the pond, native fringecups (*Tellima grandiflora*) have taken her at her word, and beside the perennial border *Corydalis ochroleuca* has inserted itself into cracks between the paving, its tiny flutes of soft cream rising from sprays of lacy leaves.

The surrounding trees and hedges, although they protect the property from the noise of busy streets nearby, also block a good deal of sunlight and their invasive roots are a constant threat to less aggressive species. The compensation for Shirley is an opportunity to indulge her love of foliage, and to echo the dapple of sunlight around the garden in complementary colours of leaf and flower. She has augmented the green and gold spring colour scheme with a carpet of starflowers, native ferns, and the low-growing Bowles' golden grass. A gloomy corner is enlivened by the sharp yellow flowers of *Kerria japonica* scattered against a grey fence, and later in summer the waxy, butter-coloured bells of *Kirengeshoma palmata* will take the stage. Closer to the house, a golden birch and a shrubby honeysuckle, *Lonicera* 'Baggeson's Gold', repeat the colour theme with their different textures.

As the season progresses, the sculptured spears of a myriad hostas rise from the ground, unfurling in shades of lime, dusky blue and spearmint green, some crisply edged or striped with cream. A perennial border emerges from behind one of the low walls. The thin branches of shrubs fill out with fresh foliage: tree peonies and roses with burgundy highlights on their new young leaves, and the acid yellow of a *Robinia pseudoacacia* 'Frisia'.

Iris bloom in the pond, and waterlilies pave the surface with their pads. Dark 'Queen of the Night' tulips rise from a bed of purple sage, and the young, silver leaves of a buddleia unfold to complement a cloudy filigree of artemisia. A brooding clump of *Anthriscus sylvestris* 'Ravenswing' in the perennial garden is echoed by a single plant in the bed on the other side of the lawn. Lupins open flower cones of striking strawberry pink or a gold and purple combination that picks up the purple of the *Anthriscus* stems. On a small paved terrace, two black iron chairs are placed where they will catch the last rays of sun on a summer evening.

As summer advances, lavenders and fragrant Mediterranean plants, passionflowers and roses, all confined behind a ribbon of clipped box hedging, bask in the warmth reflected by the south-facing wall of the house, their fragrance drifting across the patio and through the living room windows. This is the most cultivated part of the garden, close against the house. As the beds recede around the lake of green that is the lawn, the plants change to larger, wilder species, blending into the thick,

dark curtains of evergreen. Some of Shirley's "orphans," overflow from the rest of the garden, are tucked into the corners here among hostas and astilbe.

Colour schemes near the patio are muted—green, silver, purple, accented here and there with pink and blue. Red and orange are absent, except for a single pot of daylilies. Yellow is reserved for an occasional impact,

particularly in corners or far in the background under the conifers so that visitors will see a flower shining out and be drawn towards it along a path that winds among the trees. Occasionally they will find a bench placed where the view is particularly appealing, an invitation to sit a while, relax, and let the shapes, colours and scents of the garden pervade their senses. ℭ

JOHN MACKAY'S GARDEN

*"I wanted a park-like setting with some unique plants,
but also room for three young people to have
some room to play."*

FROM THE ROAD IT IS EASY TO miss the entrance to John Mackay's estate. Yet many of the drivers passing by may have wondered what is at the end of the long, curving drive that winds between banks of rhododendrons and disappears enticingly under the sweeping boughs of tall cedars, firs and maples. It emerges into a broad open landscape where the house, a solid Tudor mansion, looks south over the silver ribbon of the Fraser River to the undulating blue line of the Gulf Islands. Lines of poplars on the flat landscape still mark the sites of long-gone farmhouses.

On this side of the house the view is paramount, and planting is kept to a minimum. A semi-circle of patio and green lawn extends outward from the stone foundation, bounded by neatly clipped box and an outer screen of laurel farther down the slope. Between the two hedges, St. John's Wort (*Hypericum calycinum*) covers the

ground in a thick carpet studded with golden flowers. Swings and a tree house, beautifully crafted of polished wood in a variety of organic, curved shapes, occupy a small apron of grass on a level below the house and patio. Beyond this play area a vegetable garden steps, ziggurat-style, down the increasingly steep slope, each bed retained by a wall of weathered railway ties. In late summer tomatoes are ripening on the top level, corn standing tall on the lowest.

Having bought a nursery primarily as an investment, John Mackay developed an interest in plants and garden design through "having it rub off on me more or less unconsciously." When he moved to this property in 1986, the grounds were well-kept but lacking in interest. He began by enlisting the help of garden designer Bill Reid to renovate the area around the swimming pool, replacing old concrete with a broad terrace of

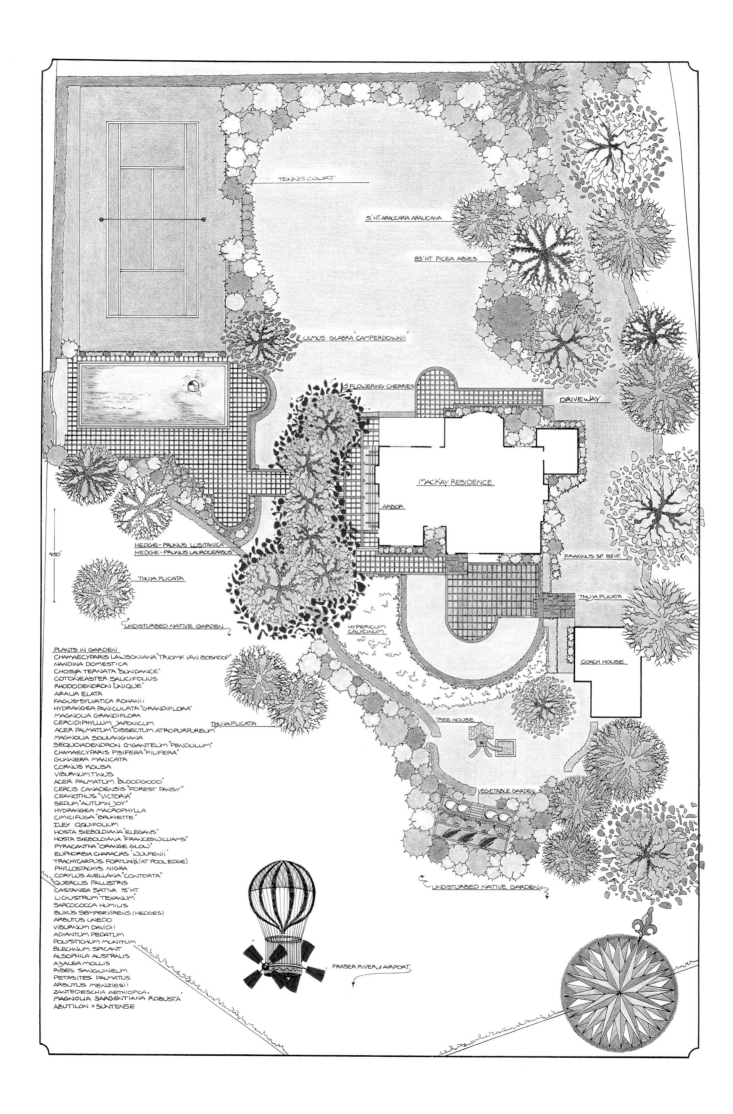

TENNIS COURT

51' HT. ARAUCARIA ARAUCANA

83' HT. PICEA ABIES

ULMUS GLABRA CAMPERDOWNII

15 FLOWERING CHERRIES

DRIVEWAY

MacKay RESIDENCE

ARBOR

FRAXINUS SP. 83' HT.

HEDGE - PRUNUS LUSITANICA
HEDGE - PRUNUS LAUROCERASUS

THUYA PLICATA

THUYA PLICATA

450'

UNDISTURBED NATIVE GARDEN

HYPERICUM CALYCINUM

COACH HOUSE

THUYA PLICATA

TREE HOUSE

VEGETABLE GARDEN

UNDISTURBED NATIVE GARDEN

PLANTS IN GARDEN
CHAMAECYPARIS LAWSONIANA "TRIOMF VAN BOSKOOP"
NANDINA DOMESTICA
CHOISYA TERNATA "SUNDANCE"
COTONEASTER SALICIFOLIUS
RHODODENDRON "UNIQUE"
ARALIA ELATA
FAGUS SYLVATICA ROHANII
HYDRANGEA PANICULATA "GRANDIFLORA"
MAGNOLIA GRANDIFLORA
CERCIDIPHYLLUM JAPONICUM
ACER PALMATUM "DISSECTUM ATROPURPUREUM"
MAGNOLIA SOULANGIANA
SEQUOIADENDRON GIGANTEUM "PENDULUM"
CHAMAECYPARIS PISIFERA "FILIFERA"
GUNNERA MANICATA
CORNUS KOUSA
VIBURNUM TINUS
ACER PALMATUM "BLOODGOOD"
CERCIS CANADENSIS "FOREST PANSY"
CEANOTHUS "VICTORIA"
SEDUM "AUTUMN JOY"
HYDRANGEA MACROPHYLLA
CIMICIFUGA "BRUNETTE"
ILEX AQUIFOLIUM
HOSTA SIEBOLDIANA "ELEGANS"
HOSTA SIEBOLDIANA "FRANCESWILLIAMS"
PYRACANTHA "ORANGE GLOW"
EUPHORBIA CHARACIAS "WULFENII"
TRACHYCARPUS FORTUNEI (AT POOL EDGE)
PHYLLOSTACHYS NIGRA
CORYLUS AVELLANA "CONTORTA"
QUERCUS PALUSTRIS
CASTANEA SATIVA 75' HT.
LIGUSTRUM "TEXANUM"
SARCOCOCCA HUMILIS
BUXUS SEMPERVIRENS (HEDGES)
ARBUTUS UNEDO
VIBURNUM DAVIDII
ADIANTUM PEDATUM
POLYSTICHUM MUNITUM
BLECHNUM SPICANT
ALSOPHILA AUSTRALIS
AZALEA MOLLIS
RIBES SANGUINEUM
PETASITES PALMATUS
ARBUTUS MENZIESII
ZANTEDESCHIA AETHIOPICA
MAGNOLIA SARGENTIANA ROBUSTA
ABUTILON x SUNTENSE

FRASER RIVER & AIRPORT

"I've tried to have different garden environments in different areas — English country around the lawn, tropical around the pool, for example."

sandstone and granite and removing some of a grove of ornamental cherries to make room for a walk to link it to the house.

Against the house, they ranged hydrangeas, plants with leaves and flowers of enough substance to balance the weight of stone around them. They met the requirement of fencing the pool area by installing an ornamental gate of black wrought iron which opens between neat clipped laurel hedges to a Mediterranean landscape of palms underplanted with *Euphorbia characias* ssp. *wulfenii,* exotic canna lilies and clusters of low-growing succulents. A gnarled Scots pine, carefully pruned to a shape suggesting brisk sea breezes, leans inward from the edge of the steep southwest slope. The rich turquoise of the pool contrasts well with the blue-grey foliage of the euphorbias and the coral blooms of *Echeveria*. At the far end of the pool, change-rooms are disguised by a colonnaded facade with a trompe-l'oeil lemon tree and oriel "windows" revealing a distant landscape. Look closely and this view resolves into distinctly west coast

conifers and mountains – not the traditional fields and oaks of the renaissance paintings it calls to mind. Clipped California lilac interspersed with columnar cedars divides the pool area from a tennis court and continues the Mediterranean illusion.

This area and the wide panorama beyond are in sharp contrast to the north side of the house where a vast expanse of lawn, groomed into a pattern of bold stripes by the attentions of a lawnmower, unrolls toward a high wall of clipped cedar. Dividing the two fields of green – one horizontal, one vertical – lies a semi-circular border of shrubs, small trees and perennials. So great is the distance from the house and so overwhelming the intensity of greenness, that large shapes and strong colours become a necessity for this planting to make an impact equal to the bulk of the house at the other end.

Graeme Bain, who has overseen the development of the garden since the Mackays took possession, has been steadily increasing the number of plants with sufficient presence to hold their own in this emerald world. Bur-

tumn Joy', whose fleshy stems have been siding with the blue-grey camp all summer, now chime in with rosy, greenish florets slowly darkening to a claret that matches the colour of the maples. A backbone of rhododendrons adds mass and substance to the composition.

At the very end of the border, the arresting silhouette of a Camperdown elm hunches over a bright scattering of red pelargoniums. Across the lawn, on the other tip of the horseshoe, a viburnum and a magnolia jostle for position, while Graeme contemplates whether to replace one or both of them with a feature tree more equal to the impact of the elm. Right now, your eye is more likely to come to rest a little farther along the curve of the border, where the imposing presence of a fine, mature monkey puzzle tree (*Araucaria araucana*) casts a long thin shadow like the hand of a sundial obliquely across the lawn.

Changes are afoot along the driveway, too, to give it more impact. *Choisya* 'Sundance', *Eucalyptus* and New Guinea impatiens have added patterns of gold, blue and bronze along its length. A huge magnolia on the edge of the ravine that marks the eastern edge of the property has been pruned into graceful layers that show off its May-blooming globes of pink and cream. It has recently acquired a partner in a young *Magnolia sargentiana* 'Robusta', planted where it can grow up to frame the gate.

John Mackay is pleased with the effect of his contributions to the estate but is quick to recognize the forethought of his predecessors, especially in planting the evergreens that frame the driveway and now, in their prime, give height and strength to the garden. "They are very important to me," he says, "as a reminder of old growth forest in the new landscape." ❧

gundy hues show well against the cedars, so Japanese maples and a *Cercis* 'Forest Pansy' are among the many layers here, their long-fingered leaves of port wine and claret mimicked by the steely blue ones of tall *Abutilon × suntense*. Around them, lavateras and Michaelmas daisies fight it out with fountains of buddleia. Close to the ground, fans of Siberian iris and frothy waves of hardy geraniums and nepeta mingle in a carefully orchestrated riot of silver, blue, pink and purple.

Graeme has taken advantage of a wet area at one end of the long border to install a *Gunnera manicata* whose giant, rough-textured leaves on stout stems continue the flow of strong structural elements out around the edges of the lawn. The pinkish tones of the flower cones at its base pick up similar hues in the flowers of an overhanging Korean dogwood (*Cornus kousa*). In fall, the effect is enriched by the strawberry-coloured fruits of the dogwood as well as the dusky rose of its turning leaves. At the same time, not far away, large clumps of *Sedum* 'Au-

PAGE 56
Blue flowers of *Ceanothus* 'Victoria' backed by the foliage of grey
Abutilon × *suntense*, maroon Cercis 'Forest Pansy' and a purple
cutleaf maple.

PAGE 57
A bronze maiden frolics in a pool of *Sedum* 'Autumn Joy'.

PAGE 59
Rhododendrons and magnolias line the driveway against a backdrop
of stately conifers.

PAGE 60
Euphorbia characias wulfenii in the warmth of the south wall.

PAGE 61
Cornus kousa, *Cercis* 'Forest Pansy', *Ceanothus* and *Acer palmatum*
against a hedge of 'Excelsa' cedar.

DEWEY AND JOHNATHAN PARKER'S GARDEN

"I like to look at the garden as a whole rather than peer at individual plants."

THE HALF-TIMBERED HOUSE, RIDING like a ship on an ocean swell of smooth green grass, looks out towards a landscape rich in deciduous trees like beeches and maples. Beyond a couple of lofty Douglas firs in the middle distance, glimpses of the Fraser River flats are visible. In the intimacy of the garden, the colours of the firs and copper beeches are repeated by the deep greens of rhododendrons and the purple feathers of Japanese maples against a backdrop of tall dark hedging. The acid lime leaves of a broadleaf maple, gleaming like pale spring sunshine, add a note of contrast which is repeated in the chartreuse leaves of nearby hostas, the brushing of gold on the dark needles of a narrow column of variegated yew, and the boldly splashed foliage of *Eleagnus pungens* 'Maculata'.

The Parkers have met the challenge of gardening on a steeply sloping site by allowing the lawn to swirl almost unbroken around the west side of the house and unroll in descending folds to the foot of the southern border. They do all the work in the garden themselves, including the meticulous mowing and edging of the beds. On the day I visited, they were engaged in trimming the massive hedge that extends the length of the southern boundary.

In the 26 years that they have lived on this property, a tradition of spending their summers on Vancouver Island has led them to develop a garden where the emphasis is on trees and shrubs with year-long appeal rather than a bright kaleidoscope of summer-blooming perennials. Using the textures of foliage, the silhouettes of branch and tree-trunk, and a palette confined predominantly to gold, burgundy and all shades of green from dark jade to silver-grey, they have composed a serene landscape. The rolling swells of green lawn are

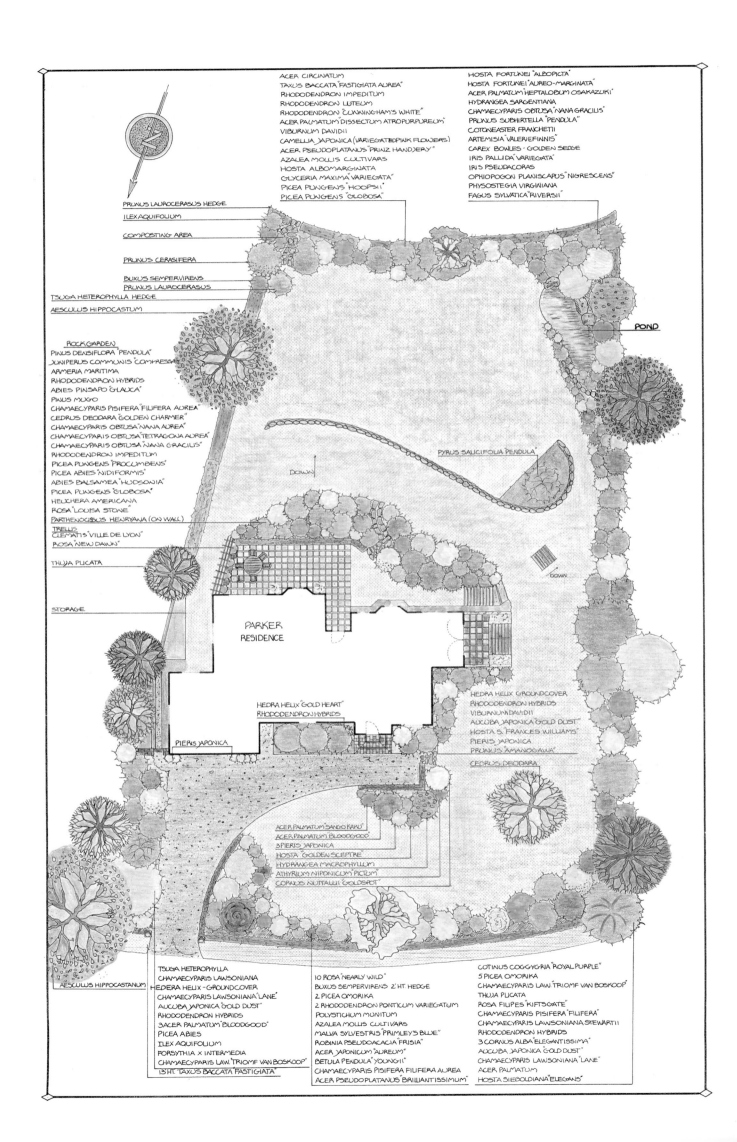

"This garden isn't meant to have a perennial border. There's no place where you can get that long look down a border that is the best view."

repeated in the plump blue seersucker folds of hosta leaves; the downy, dark grey foliage of *Hydrangea sargentiana* finds an echo in the pale fleece of *Stachys byzantina*; fine slivers of *Glyceria maxima*, an ornamental grass, complement the delicate lace of a cutleaf Japanese maple. Along the edge of the steepest fold of lawn, a low wall of soft grey stone ends in an arabesque around the silver elegance of a weeping willow-leaved pear tree. Beneath its dappled canopy the white flower spikes and pewter leaves of *Hosta sieboldiana* var. *elegans* continue the metallic colour theme.

In the upper garden behind the house, colour contrasts are more dramatic. The bright lemon foliage of

Robinia pseudoacacia 'Frisia', isolated in a frame of emerald lawn, finds reflections in the flecked leaves of a variegated *Aucuba japonica* against the house, and in the golden circles of a full-moon maple. The sheer face of the moody yew hedge along the sidewalk is scrawled with a pattern of golden hops, and across the lawn, from its vantage point on the wall beside the door, 'Gold Heart' ivy flashes anwering beams of light. Where the driveway makes its short curve towards the house, a pair of Serbian spruce rise like lances against the sky. A screen of *Rhododendron* 'Vulcan', salvaged from a demolition site, encloses the end of the garden and enlivens the composition with flame-red flowers in spring.

To take advantage of the views to the south, the Parkers have recently added a sunroom to the east side of the house and laid a terrace of greenish slate. Climbing roses—'Morning Jewel' against the house and the pale pink blossoms of 'New Dawn' on an adjoining lattice—will give soft colour to the surroundings and blend with the creams and pale browns of the house. Stone troughs imported from Provence are already overflowing with succulents, and a collection of urns and pots gives Dewey a chance to experiment with seasonal combinations of texture and variations on monochrome themes.

Under the living room windows, Dewey has planted a hundred 'Apricot Beauty' tulip bulbs—a sheet of colour on the ground in spring—and apricot roses below the terrace carry the same hue forward into summer. Later in the summer, an obelisk at the head of steps leading down to the lower lawn glows with the ruby stars of *Clematis* 'Gravetye Beauty'.

Although numerous plants in this garden are unusual enough to attract a collector's eye, the Parkers are first and foremost designers, constantly reworking their canvas to improve the long views from terrace or gateway. Recently, they have replaced a hemlock hedge along their eastern boundary with *Thuja* 'Emerald Giant', a particularly vivid and healthy variety of cedar, and plans are afoot to shift the full-moon maple to where a faltering dogwood now grows. Boxwood which used to line the driveway now delineates the edge of the new terrace, and relocated kurume azaleas occupy the slope below.

They are talking about adding movement to the pond to make it more of a feature, and have plans for an arbour on the other side of the lawn to shelter a garden seat. On the other hand, they are also flirting with the temptation of finding some acreage outside the city and starting all over again, influenced by a different *genius loci*. ❧

PAGE 62
Foliage highlights around a waterlily pond.

PAGE 63
Dwarf conifers *Pinus mugo* and *Cedrus deodara* 'Golden Charmer' and *Rhododendron impeditum* frame a statue.

PAGE 65
Golden yews (*Taxus baccata* 'Fastigiata Aurea') behind a border of hardy geraniums, astilbe and lambs' ears (*Stachys byzantina*).

PAGE 66–67
Golden foliage of *Chamaecyparis lawsoniana* 'Lane' and blue leaves of *Hosta sieboldiana* 'Elegans' complement the pink flowers of *Geranium sanguineum*.

PAGE 67 ABOVE
Chamaecyparis lawsoniana 'Lane' finds an echo in *Robinia pseudo-acacia* 'Frisia'.

CLAIRE AND JAMIE WRIGHT'S GARDEN

"I like to clad things, to have lots of things that overhang. I'm a messy person at heart."

OLD SHAUGHNESSY IS THE CLOSEST young Vancouver comes to a historic "nob hill" area. Developed by the Canadian Pacific Railway into a neighbourhood of grand buildings and curving, tree-lined boulevards, it has preserved its gracious demeanour and old-money atmosphere against a century of threats. Properties change hands slowly.

Claire and Jamie Wright are the fourth owners of the house where they have lived for 18 years. A stern mansion with heavy stone battlements and an imposing porch, it occupies the high ground facing north to the coast mountains beyond the towers of the downtown city. A tall Japanese umbrella pine (*Sciadopitys verticillata*) anchors its northwest corner and a row of large, dark-leaved rhododendrons hugs the walls under long, mullioned windows. A massive catalpa leans from the neighbour's garden to throw its broad shadow across the semi-circle of drive. When the Wrights moved in, little else was there but unbroken lawn—in cold winters, their children flooded the front yard for use as a skating rink.

Now, where they once held impromptu hockey matches, a mixed border of astilbe, hostas, peonies, roses, fall asters and phlox surrounds geometric beds edged with the traditional boxwood. In the centre, clouds of blue-flowered nepeta encircle a weathered stone fountain and the rectangular beds on either side are full of white 'Iceberg' roses. A young yew hedge is beginning to hide the railings along the sidewalk and muffle the sound of traffic on nearby streets.

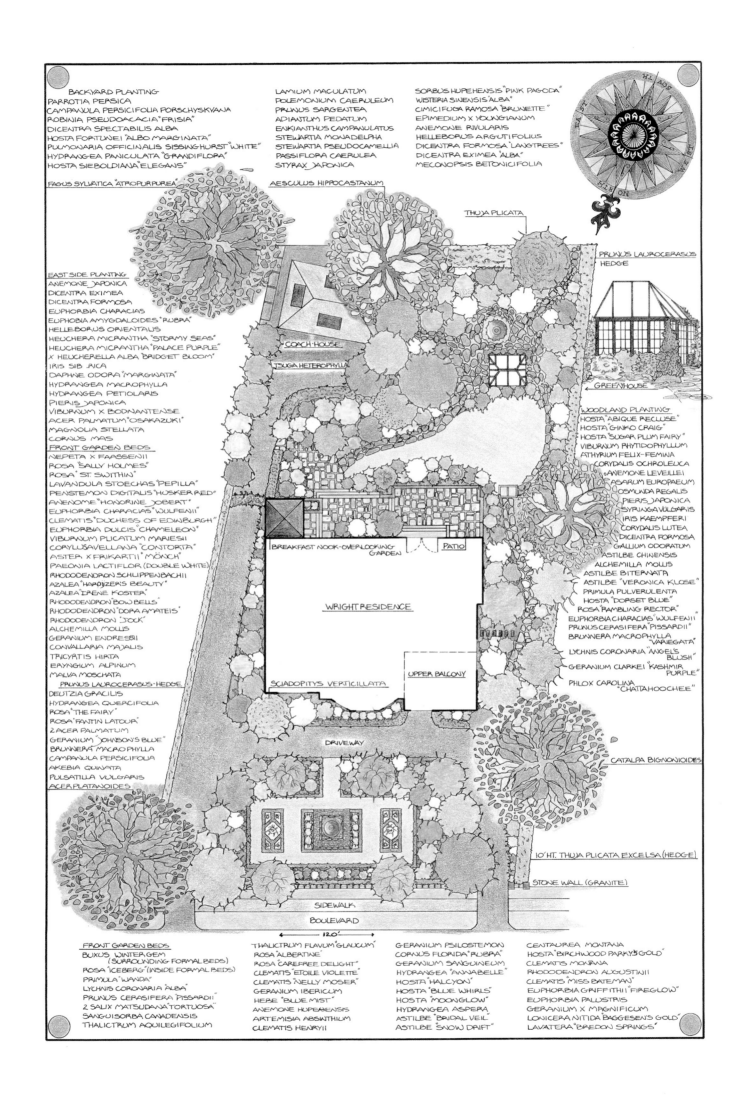

Within these formal outlines, shapes are flowing and colours are muted. Claire loves the effect of masses of pale colour, beginning in early spring with a sea of small bulbs, china blue *Chionodoxa luciliae* and darker grape hyacinth (*Muscari armeniacum*), washing around the feet of the lilacs that flank the entrance to the garden. Lemon snouts of *Hosta* 'Moonglow' and 'Halcyon' emerge like dolphins through the rippled surface. The scent of Exbury azaleas drifts on the air, white varieties along the fence and creamy peach-coloured 'Irene Koster' where it can perfume the driveway, mingling with the lilacs. More perfume comes from clumps of

white *Narcissus* 'Thalia' underneath the azaleas.

As the season changes, Korean dogwoods cloak themselves in pink-flushed white flowers, and the shady east side of the garden, dominated by a huge maple, carpets itself in ferns, steely blue hostas and ivory plumes of astilbe. Farther out in the sunshine, Oriental poppy 'Mrs. Perry's White' opens its wide bowls to show the purple velvet boss of stamens inside, the 'Iceberg' roses begin to bloom and *Clematis* 'Miss Bateman' twines strands of white stars around the dogwood trunks. By early fall, the lilac flowers of meadow rue (*Thalictrum aquilegifolium*) have given way to phlox and fall asters in similar hues, and the foliage of the dogwoods is beginning to take on the same rosy tints as flowers of 'The Fairy' roses.

Behind the house, a similar pageant has taken place, the players here being hardy geraniums in shades of blue, the pleated leaves of lady's mantle and Bowles' golden grass (*Milium effusum* 'Aureum'), which delights Claire with the way it "shimmers and rustles in every breath of wind." An arch leading to the garage is heavily festooned with pink-flowering 'Albertine' and 'New Dawn' roses as well as a vigorous white clematis. Focal point for this garden is a small but dramatic gothic glasshouse, its wooden frame painted in the same glossy black as the trim on the house. A young *Parthenocissus* crawls up one corner and an *Akebia quinata* drapes the back wall. Recently constructed by Jamie, it already has a deceptive air of antiquity about it. Jamie also laid the flagstones of Whistler basalt that loop around the remaining teardrop of lawn and pave a small, mossy courtyard behind the greenhouse, where a

crumbling fountain, an ornament inherited with the property, sits in a bed of white violets, lady's mantle, white-splashed *Pulmonaria* 'Roy Davidson' and white bleeding heart. In keeping with the green and white theme, Claire has planted white Emperor tulips, variegated hostas, sweet woodruff and white azaleas in the surrounding beds. A *Robinia pseudoacacia* 'Frisia' shines like a golden lamp among the cool colours.

From the wide stone terrace, which they built to blend with the house, the Wrights can admire the fruits of their labours across a series of elegant planters overflowing with *Lobelia* 'Cambridge Blue', *Helichrysum* 'Limelight' and pale pink pelargoniums. The border directly below is thick with nepeta, peonies, euphorbias, pink astilbe and phlox. Breaking away from her favourite pastels, Claire has planted a large clump of gloriosa daisies (*Rudbeckia hirta*) to add strength to this composition and the golden yellow petals with their black centres add warmth and vitality to the soft tones of pink and lavender that surround them.

West of the terrace, a black-painted arch, overhung with *Rosa* 'Rambling Rector', echoes the steep roof of the greenhouse. It leads to a quiet, shady garden at the side of the house where a huge *Viburnum opulus* becomes a canopy of white in May. Beneath its shelter, Claire has planted myriad bulbs of sky-blue grape hyacinth, which bloom among the unfolding fans of hostas. Across the way, a *Kirengeshoma palmata* holds globules of butter-yellow flowers on arching stems

beneath the knobby trunk of an ancient mock orange. An equally elderly crab-apple shoulders its way up beside the wall of the house. Claire and Jamie have pruned it like a giant espalier, moulding its hoary arms to the same curve as the arched openings of the front porch.

On the other side of the house, a huge wisteria nudges against the eaves and pokes enquiring tendrils through the upstairs windows. Around its feet, wedged between the wall and the drive, is Claire's "red garden," an experiment still in progress. Much of the colour comes from the dark and dappled leaves of heucheras like 'Stormy Seas' and 'Pewter Veil', which she likes as much for their names as for their colourful appearance, and the spurge family, especially *Euphorbia amygdaloides* 'Rubra'. A *Pieris japonica,* one of the few shrubs that pre-date the Wrights' occupancy, now shares its territory with a dark red astilbe and a maroon azalea, all yielding in fall to the brilliance of Japanese maple 'Osakazuki', noted for the intensity of its fall colour.

On either side of the drive as it extends to the back of the property, a dense carpet of *Geranium maccrorhizum* covers the ground. With six children in the family Claire describes this as "a good plant for surviving learner-drivers." Above rise three flowering cherries, their lime-coloured leaves hung with pale drops of pink in spring. Bought as tiny saplings, they have been trimmed as they grew to reveal the beauty of their trunks and dapple the ground with their leafy shadows where they overhang the driveway.

Here as elsewhere, the combination of carefully pruned trees and luxuriant underplanting gives the garden an air of permanence, yet much of the landscape behind the house is less than five years old. As their children have grown, and their need for a playground has diminished, the parents have gradually reclaimed more of the outdoor space and, with a growing passion for gardening, turned it into an absorbing playground of their own. ❧

DEBORAH GIBSON'S GARDEN

"I like the process of finding out what the shapes of the plants are, what combinations work. That's gardening for me."

When the Gibsons moved to their present house in South Shaughnessy, the wide lawn that faced the street was bordered on either side by an impenetrable wall of green shrubbery—mostly overgrown laurels and 'Unique' rhododendrons, or "Hardly Unique" as Deborah likes to call them. Most of the laurels are gone now, and the rhododendrons are part of a mixed shrub border between the sidewalk and a low brick wall that encloses and secludes the garden. It was a deliberate move to set the wall far enough inside the property line so that there would be space for planting outside "to give back to the street." An underplanting of pink *Geranium endressii* echoes the pink flowers of the rhododendrons, and a vigorous clematis twines through their leathery leaves. In winter the scent of *Heptacodium jasminoides*

wafts over the sidewalk, succeeded in summer by the fragrance of climbing roses leaning over the wall.

A giant Douglas fir stands sentinel where the path to the front door begins, its trunk wreathed in the blue flowers of *Campanula portenschlagiana*. *Erysimum* 'Bowles' Mauve' is also content in this patch of soil sucked dry by the tree's roots.

Inside the wall a Japanese maple and a rhododendron remain from the old scheme, with saxifrages, ferns and trilliums growing through the moss that flourishes in their shade.

To guide her in the initial renovation of the garden Deborah retained Michael Luco, well-known in Vancouver for his graceful designs. The linear arrangement of flower beds enclosing exuberant plantings and the use of contrasting hard surfaces of stone and weathered

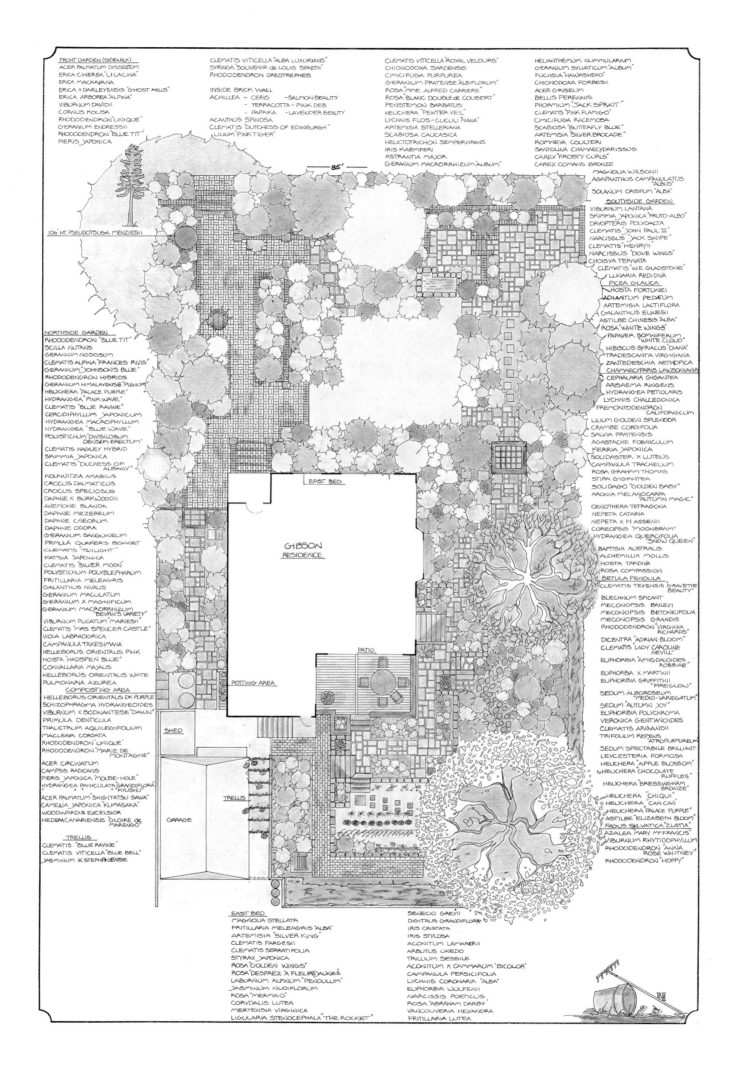

FRONT GARDEN (SIDEWALK)
ACER PALMATUM DISSECTUM
ERICA CINEREA "LI LACINA"
ERICA MACKAYANA
ERICA X DARLEYENSIS "GHOST HILLS"
ERICA ARBOREA "ALPINA"
VIBURNUM DAVIDII
CORNUS KOUSA
RHODODENDRON "UNIQUE"
GERANIUM ENDRESSII
RHODODENDRON "BLUE TIT"
PIERIS JAPONICA

INSIDE BRICK WALL
ACHILLEA — CERIS — SALMON BEAUTY
        — TERRACOTTA — PINK DEB
        — PAPRIKA — LAVENDER BEAUTY
ACANTHUS SPINOSA
CLEMATIS "DUTCHESS OF EDINBURGH"
LILIUM "PINK TIGER"

CLEMATIS VITICELLA "ALBA LUXURIANS"
SYRINGA "SOUVENIR de LOUIS SPAETH"
RHODODENDRON OREOTREPHES

CLEMATIS VITICELLA "ROYAL VELOURS"
CHIONODOXA SARDENSIS
CIMICIFUGA PURPUREA
GERANIUM PRATENSE "ALBIFLORUM"
ROSA "MME. ALFRED CARRIERE"
ROSA "BLANC DOUBLE de COUBERT"
PENSTEMON BARBATUS
HEUCHERA "PEWTER VEIL"
LYCHNIS FLOS-CUCULI "NANA"
ARTEMISIA STELLERIANA
SCABIOSA CAUCASICA
HELICTOTRICHON SEMPERVIRENS
IRIS KAEMFERI
ASTRANTIA MAJOR
GERANIUM MACRORRHIZUM "ALBUM"

HELIANTHEMUM NUMMULARIUM
GERANIUM SYLVATICUM "ALBUM"
FUCHSIA "HAWKSHEAD"
CHIONODOXA FORBESII
ACER GRISEUM
BELLIS PERENNIS
PHORMIUM "JACK SPRATT"
CLEMATIS "PINK FLAMIGO"
CIMICIFUGA RACEMOSA
SCABIOSA "BUTTERFLY BLUE"
ARTEMISIA "SILVER BROCADE"
ROMNEYA COULTERI
SANTOLINA CHAMAECYPARISSUS
CAREX "FROSTY CURLS"
CAREX COMANS BRONZE

MAGNOLIA WILSONII
AGAPANTHUS CAMPANULATUS "ALBUS"
SOLANUM CRISPUM "ALBA"

SOUTHSIDE GARDEN
VIBURNUM LANTANA
SKIMMIA JAPONICA "FRUTO-ALBO"
DRYOPTERIS POLYDACTA
CLEMATIS "JOHN PAUL II"
NARCISSUS "JACK SNIPE"
CLEMATIS "HENRYI"
NARCISSUS "DOVE WINGS"
CHOISYA TERNATA
CLEMATIS "W.E. GLADSTONE"
LUNARIA REDIVIVA
PICEA GLAUCA
HOSTA FORTUNEI
ADIANTUM PEDATUM
ARTEMISIA LACTIFLORA
GALANTHUS ELWESII
ASTILBE CHINESIS "ALBA"
ROSA "WHITE WINGS"
PAPAVER SOMNIFERUM "WHITE CLOUD"
HIBISCUS SYRIACUS "DIANA"
TRADESCANTIA VIRGINIANA
ZANTEDESCHIA AETHIOPICA
CHAMAECYPARIS LAWSONIANA
CEPHALARIA GIGANTEA
ARISAEMA RINGENS
HYDRANGEA PETIOLARIS
LYCHNIS CHALCEDONICA
FREMONTODENDRON CALIFORNICUM
LILIUM GOLDEN SPLENDOR
CRAMBE CORDIFOLIA
SALVIA PRATENSIS
AGASTACHE FOENICULUM
KERRIA JAPONICA
SOLIDASTER X LUTEUS
CAMPANULA TRACHELIUM
ROSA GRAHAM THOMAS
STIPA GIGANTEA
SOLIDAGO "GOLDEN BABY"
ARONIA MELANOCARPA "AUTUMN MAGIC"
OENOTHERA TETRAGONA
NEPETA CATARIA
NEPETA X FI ASSENII
COREOPSIS "MOONBEAM"
HYDRANGEA QUERCIFOLIA "SNOW QUEEN"
BAPTISIA AUSTRALIS
ALCHEMILLA MOLLIS
HOSTA TARDIVA
ROSA COMPASSION
BETULA PENDULA
CLEMATIS TEXENSIS "GRAVETYE BEAUTY"
BLECHNUM SPICANT
MECONOPSIS BAILEYI
MECONOPSIS BETONICIFOLIA
MECONOPSIS GRANDIS
RHODODENDRON "VIRGINIA RICHARDS"
DICENTRA "ADRIAN BLOOM"
CLEMATIS "LADY CAROLINE NEVILL"
EUPHORBIA "AMYGDALOIDES ROBBIAE"
EUPHORBIA X MARTINII
EUPHORBIA GRIFFITHII "FIREGLOW"
SEDUM ALBOROSEUM "MEDIO-VARIEGATUM"
SEDUM "AUTUMN JOY"
EUPHORBIA POLYCHROMA
VERONICA GENTIANOIDES
CLEMATIS ARMANDII
TRIFOLIUM REPENS "ATROPURPUREM"
SEDUM SPECTABILE BRILLIANT
LEYCESTERIA FORMOSA
HEUCHERA "APPLE BLOSSOM"
HEUCHERA "CHOCOLATE RUFFLES"
HEUCHERA "BRESSINGHAM BRONZE"
HEUCHERA "CHIQUI"
HEUCHERA "CAN CAN"
HEUCHERA "PALACE PURPLE"
ASTILBE "ELIZABETH BLOOM"
FAGUS SILVATICA "ZLATIA"
AZALEA MARY McFRANCIS
VIBURNUM RHYTIDOPHYLLUM
RHODODENDRON "ANNA ROSE WHITNEY"
RHODODENDRON "HOPPY"

NORTHSIDE GARDEN
RHODODENDRON "BLUE TIT"
SCILLA NUTANS
GERANIUM NODOSUM
CLEMATIS ALPINA "FRANCES RIVIS"
GERANIUM "JOHNSON'S BLUE"
RHODODENDRON HYBRIDS
GERANIUM HIMALAYENSE "PLENUM"
HEUCHERA "PALACE PURPLE"
HYDRANGEA "PINK WAVE"
CLEMATIS "BLUE RAVINE"
CERCIDIPHYLLUM JAPONICUM
HYDRANGEA MACROPHYLLUM
HYDRANGEA "BLUE WAVE"
POLYSTICHUM "DIVISILOBUM DENSUM ERECTUM"
CLEMATIS HAGLEY HYBRID
SKIMMIA JAPONICA
CLEMATIS "DUCHESS OF ALBANY"
KOLKWITZIA AMABILIS
CROCUS DALMATICUS
CROCUS SPECIOSUS
DAPHNE X BURKWOODII
ANEMONE BLANDA
DAPHNE MEZEREUM
DAPHNE CNEORUM
DAPHNE ODORA
GERANIUM SANGUINEUM
PRIMULA QUAKER'S BONNET
CLEMATIS "TWILIGHT"
FATSIA JAPONICA
CLEMATIS "SILVER MOON"
POLYSTICHUM POLYBLEPHARUM
FRITILLARIA MELEAGRIS
GALANTHUS NIVALIS
GERANIUM MACULATUM
GERANIUM X MAGNIFICUM
GERANIUM MACRORRHIZUM "BEVAN'S VARIETY"
VIBURNUM PLICATUM "MARIESII"
CLEMATIS "MRS SPENCER CASTLE"
VIOLA LABRADORICA
CAMPANULA TAKESIMANA
HELLEBORUS ORIENTALIS PINK
HOSTA "HADSPEN BLUE"
CONVALLARIA MAJALIS
HELLEBORUS ORIENTALIS WHITE
PULMONARIA AZUREA
COMPOSTING AREA
HELLEBORUS ORIENTALIS DK PURPLE
SCHIZOPHRAGMA HYDRANGEOIDES
VIBURNUM X BODNANTESE "DAWN"
PRIMULA DENTICULA
THALICTRUM AQUILEGIFOLIUM
MACLEAYA CORDATA
RHODODENDRON "UNIQUE"
RHODODENDRON "MARIE DE MONTAGNE"

ACER CIRCINATUM
CAMPSIS RADICANS
PIERIS JAPONICA "MOUSE-HOLE"
HYDRANGEA PANICULATA GRANDIFLORA "KYUSHU"
ACER PALMATUM SHIGITATSU SAWA
CAMELLIA JAPONICA "KUMASAKA"
WOODWARDIA EXCELSIOR
HEDERA CANARIENSIS "GLOIRE de MARENGO"

TRELLIS
CLEMATIS "BLUE RAVINE"
CLEMATIS VITICELLA "BLUE BELL"
JASMINUM X STEPHANENSE

85'

106' HT. PSEUDOTSUGA MENZIESII

EAST BED

GIBSON RESIDENCE

PATIO

POTTING AREA

SHED

GARAGE

TRELLIS

EAST BED
MAGNOLIA STELLATA
FRITILLARIA MELEAGRIS "ALBA"
ARTEMISIA "SILVER KING"
CLEMATIS FARGESII
CLEMATIS SERRATIFOLIA
STYRAX JAPONICA
ROSA "GOLDEN WINGS"
ROSA "DESPREZ A FLEURS JAUNES"
LABURNUM ALPINUM "PENDULUM"
JASMINUM NUDIFLORUM
ROSA "MERMAID"
CORYDALIS LUTEA
MERTENSIA VIRGINICA
LIGULARIA STENOCEPHALA "THE ROCKET"

SENECIO GREYII
DIGITALIS GRANDIFLORA
IRIS CRISTATA
IRIS STYLOSA
ACONITUM LAMARCKII
ARBUTUS UNEDO
TRILLIUM SESSILE
ACONITUM X CAMMARUM "BICOLOR"
CAMPANULA PERSICIFOLIA
LYCHNIS CORONARIA "ALBA"
EUPHORBIA WULFENII
NARCISSIS POETICUS
ROSA "ABRAHAM DARBY"
VANCOUVERIA HEXANDRA
FRITILLARIA LUTEA

"What I'm aiming for is all-season interest. At the same time, I've come to realize that plants look best when they are grouped to bloom at the same time."

brick are Luco signatures. His influence is also recognizable in a rectangular pond of pea-green, opaque water, speared by slender lances of bulrushes, its grey stone coping surrounded by a flurry of silver foliage. The sound of water bubbling from its fountain masks the traffic noises beyond the wall, making a peaceful refuge of the sunlit corner where Deborah likes to sit and observe the change of patterns in her white garden that encloses the small paved space. The succession of blooms here, in the dark shadow of a large viburnum, begins with crocuses and pale hellebores followed by the luminous flowers of *Camellia* 'Silver Wings' and a white azalea. In June, white roses dominate and are superseded in their turn, first by 'Casablanca' lilies and then by *Anemone* 'Honorine Jobert' and *Hibiscus syriacus* 'Diana'. In the background, *Magnolia wilsonii* hangs its waxen lamps in late spring and *Clematis* 'Huldine' twines along the fence from summer into fall.

Deborah admits to "an insatiable greed for plants" and is always buying another treasure. She keeps a list on her computer of all her acquisitions, along with their preferred conditions, good companion plants, and a map of their location in the garden. The result of her interest in individual specimens has led to what she terms "drifts of one," especially in the newer parts of the garden, but in the older plantings she is beginning to group more plants together and to pursue colour themes, such as the border of silver, blue and gold flowers that runs along the front of the house.

Around the side of the house a lych gate leads into to a different atmosphere. Although south-facing, the unusually wide side garden is heavily dappled by the trailing fingers of a lovely old birch and shaded by a high backdrop of evergreens interlaced with clematis. Here, from his basement study, William Gibson, noted author of such cyber-punk novels as *Neuromancer* and *Mona Lisa Overdrive* can look up from his labours over what his wife refers to as "Bill's garden of enigmas." For his entertainment she has filled the plot under the windows with oddities like a weirdly contorted *Pieris*, a clutch of reptilian *Arisaema*, some strange little bonsai evergreens and the brain-like blobs of puffball mushrooms.

More conservative shade-lovers like *Heuchera*, *Tiarella* and their combined offspring, *Heucherella*, fill the other beds, along with hardy geraniums. Himalayan blue poppies thrive under the birch.

At the back of the house a series of terraces bounded by low stone balustrades drops from house to ground level. The house is set well to the back of the property and space is limited here. It was even more confined by a massive cypress hedge when the Gibsons arrived, but as the cypress were slowly dying, Deborah reluctantly had them removed. The bonus was an extra eight feet of open ground in which to expand the garden. The area is still in transition—particularly a vegetable plot being rethought in light of the resident cats' fondness for digging in it. Meanwhile a froth of annuals is giving temporary colour.

In the deepest darkest corner of the backyard, a rustic swinging seat beneath a magnificent beech is another of Deborah's favourite places for reading and reflection. From this point she can look straight along the path that runs from back to front of the property, through the arch of the gate and successive layers of shifting, changing colour, all the way to the seat at the base of the front wall. It is a very literal interpretation of "taking the long view," and one which gives her great pleasure. Ꮸ

PAGE 74
Rose 'Paul Lédé flowers on a gate between front and back gardens.

PAGE 75
Himalayan blue poppy (*Meconopsis betonifolia*).

PAGE 77
Spiky blue grasses (*Helictotrichon sempervirens* and *Festuca glauca*) around the pond in the front garden.

PAGE 78
A collection of pots holds sedums and sempervivums.

PAGE 79
Ferns, including *Athyrium japonicum pictum* and *Blechnum spicant*, thrive in the shade cast by a golden beech and weeping birch.

BRENDA PETERSON'S GARDEN

"There is no plan. Having a plan would spoil the fun."

BETWEEN A WHITE PICKET FENCE and the tall, shingled, Edwardian house, painted a soft dove grey with burgundy trim, the small garden overflows with a cottage mixture of trees, shrubs and perennials. The corner lot in Kitsilano stops cars in the street outside, and joggers slow to a walk to admire the view.

"It was a lost garden," Brenda says of the corner lot that she and husband Basil Stuart-Stubbs bought some 13 years ago, "just grass and some poppies." She knew little about plants back then; what had drawn them to the property was the potential of the beautiful but neglected house, and its proximity to the university where they both worked as librarians.

"Then I happened to go to a Vancouver Rose Society show," Brenda recalls. "I joined the society and won the door prize at my first meeting. It was an omen." One of the first roses she planted, the soft pink climber 'New Dawn', now drapes the south side of the house from eaves to ground level. At its feet, clusters of smaller but richer pink blooms adorn 'The Fairy,' a shrub rose listed in catalogues as "short-growing," but easily rising to shoulder height in this sunny, sheltered spot. By the fence are more roses—'Penelope' and 'Buff Beauty', hybrid musk roses that flower summer and fall with sweetly scented petals the colour of old lace. In a nearby corner 'Madame Alfred Carrière', a fragrant white noisette rose, hangs in drifts from the branches of a huge old dogwood, leaning out over the sidewalk.

Brenda's passion for gardening and the influence of her career have led to the acquisition of a formidable

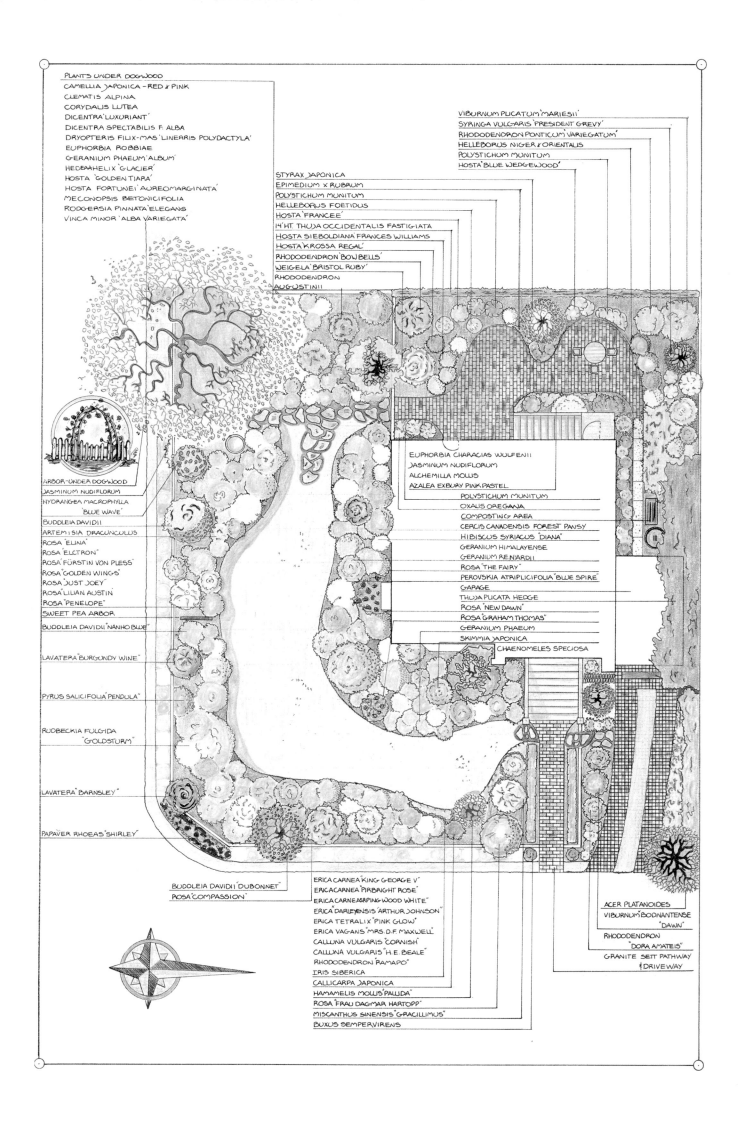

PLANTS UNDER DOGWOOD
CAMELLIA JAPONICA - RED & PINK
CLEMATIS ALPINA
CORYDALIS LUTEA
DICENTRA 'LUXURIANT'
DICENTRA SPECTABILIS F. ALBA
DRYOPTERIS FILIX-MAS 'LINEARIS POLYDACTYLA'
EUPHORBIA ROBBIAE
GERANIUM PHAEUM 'ALBUM'
HEDERA HELIX 'GLACIER'
HOSTA 'GOLDEN TIARA'
HOSTA FORTUNEI 'AUREOMARGINATA'
MECONOPSIS BETONICIFOLIA
RODGERSIA PINNATA 'ELEGANS'
VINCA MINOR 'ALBA VARIEGATA'

VIBURNUM PLICATUM 'MARIESII'
SYRINGA VULGARIS 'PRESIDENT GREVY'
RHODODENDRON PONTICUM 'VARIEGATUM'
HELLEBORUS NIGER & ORIENTALIS
POLYSTICHUM MUNITUM
HOSTA 'BLUE WEDGEWOOD'

STYRAX JAPONICA
EPIMEDIUM X RUBRUM
POLYSTICHUM MUNITUM
HELLEBORUS FOETIDUS
HOSTA 'FRANCEE'
14' HT. THUJA OCCIDENTALIS FASTIGIATA
HOSTA SIEBOLDIANA 'FRANCES WILLIAMS'
HOSTA 'KROSSA REGAL'
RHODODENDRON 'BOW BELLS'
WEIGELA 'BRISTOL RUBY'
RHODODENDRON
AUGUSTINII

ARBOR UNDER DOGWOOD
JASMINUM NUDIFLORUM
HYDRANGEA MACROPHYLLA
   'BLUE WAVE'
BUDDLEIA DAVIDII
ARTEMISIA DRACUNCULUS
ROSA 'ELINA'
ROSA 'ELECTRON'
ROSA 'FÜRSTIN VON PLESS'
ROSA 'GOLDEN WINGS'
ROSA 'JUST JOEY'
ROSA 'LILIAN AUSTIN'
ROSA 'PENELOPE'
SWEET PEA ARBOR
BUDDLEIA DAVIDII 'NANHO BLUE'

LAVATERA 'BURGUNDY WINE'

PYRUS SALICIFOLIA 'PENDULA'

RUDBECKIA FULGIDA
   'GOLDSTURM'

LAVATERA 'BARNSLEY'

PAPAVER RHOEAS 'SHIRLEY'

EUPHORBIA CHARACIAS WULFENII
JASMINUM NUDIFLORUM
ALCHEMILLA MOLLIS
AZALEA EXBURY PINK PASTEL
POLYSTICHUM MUNITUM
OXALIS OREGANA
COMPOSTING AREA
CERCIS CANADENSIS FOREST PANSY
HIBISCUS SYRIACUS 'DIANA'
GERANIUM HIMALAYENSE
GERANIUM RENARDII
ROSA 'THE FAIRY'
PEROVSKIA ATRIPLICIFOLIA 'BLUE SPIRE'
GARAGE
THUJA PLICATA HEDGE
ROSA 'NEW DAWN'
ROSA 'GRAHAM THOMAS'
GERANIUM PHAEUM
SKIMMIA JAPONICA
CHAENOMELES SPECIOSA

BUDDLEIA DAVIDII 'DUBONNET'
ROSA 'COMPASSION'

ERICA CARNEA 'KING GEORGE V'
ERICA CARNEA 'PIRBRIGHT ROSE'
ERICA CARNEA 'SPRING WOOD WHITE'
ERICA DARLEYENSIS 'ARTHUR JOHNSON'
ERICA TETRALIX 'PINK GLOW'
ERICA VAGANS 'MRS. D.F. MAXWELL'
CALLUNA VULGARIS 'CORNISH'
CALLUNA VULGARIS 'H.E. BEALE'
RHODODENDRON 'RAMAPO'
IRIS SIBERICA
CALLICARPA JAPONICA
HAMAMELIS MOLLIS 'PALLIDA'
ROSA 'FRAU DAGMAR HARTOPP'
MISCANTHUS SINENSIS 'GRACILLIMUS'
BUXUS SEMPERVIRENS

ACER PLATANOIDES
VIBURNUM BODNANTENSE
   'DAWN'
RHODODENDRON
   'DORA AMATEIS'
GRANITE SETT PATHWAY
& DRIVEWAY

personal library of books on plants and garden design. The knowledge she absorbs from her reading has been translated into a garden where there is drama at every season. Early in the year, the creamy bells of a white-flowering currant grace the driveway, and sulphur-coloured, spidery blossoms of witch hazel infuse the air with their elusive, bittersweet scent. Beneath the wide branches of the dogwood, pink tulips emerge above a drift of ferns, bleeding hearts and sweet woodruff.

Late spring brings flowers on rhododendrons and azaleas, and in summer the roses, now 27 in number, bloom in watercolour shades among catmints, hardy geraniums, lupins, delphiniums, clematis, valerian and a host of other perennials, including the poppies from long ago, all punctuated by the blue of cornflowers and tall spires of hollyhocks in lemon yellow and deep burgundy.

Asters and Japanese anemones herald the fall, along with penstemons and the wine-coloured heads of *Sedum* 'Autumn Joy', and in winter heaths and heathers have their moment beneath the silver leaves of *Buddleia* 'Dubonnet'. Brenda likes to leave its stark outline until spring before cutting it back hard to encourage strong new growth. The fruits of a beautyberry (*Callicarpa japonica*) cluster like round purple candies on its leafless branches from November through the new year. It also gets severely pruned each spring to keep it small enough to fit into its allotted space. Behind it, the fat red hips of rugosa rose 'Fru Dagmar Hartopp' bulge like cherry tomatoes as its leaves turn from green to gold and gradually drop away. As December begins, the bright berries of a viburnum shine out from the gloom under the dogwood like Christmas lights.

Three years ago, the couple embarked on a major renovation of the area behind the house. This small rectangular space shaded on all sides by trees and walls

has become a green haven where the heavy, textured leaves of hostas contrast with lacy ferns. Colour comes mainly from subtle hues of foliage, such as the marbled leaves of *Heuchera* 'Pewter Veil' and 'Palace Purple', or from the pale petals of hellebores. The bells of foxgloves and the silky feathers of astilbes seem brighter than usual when they bloom in this cool oasis. On hot summer afternoons this is a favourite place for Brenda and Basil to retreat with their ever-present books and magazines.

More recently, the driveway was repaved and edged with a row of dwarf boxwood. "I'd tried a number of different groundcovers, like kinnickinnick, and *Genista* 'Vancouver Gold', says Brenda, "but in the winter, people didn't notice they were there and walked over them. They had a hard time surviving." After considering and rejecting a number of different options, she chose an *Enkianthus* for the prime position beside the porch steps, where its odd little bells in bleached yellow and pink can be admired from close at hand.

The picket fence now makes a right angle alongside the driveway and a new gate opens onto the short path to the front steps. Beside the gate, Brenda's signature poppies and fragrant tufts of dame's rocket (*Hesperis matronalis*) spill out towards the sidewalk between the slats of the fence.

Conscientious librarian that she is, Brenda keeps a computer record of her plants, updating it regularly whenever she adds to her collection. This is a constant task as she is always on the lookout for new and unusual plants, although a certain amount of juggling is required to fit her purchases into a garden already so bountiful. Prime position on the corner of the house used to be held by *Hamamelis* 'Diane', which was ousted a couple of years ago by *Cercis* 'Forest Pansy'. Last winter, 'Forest Pansy' moved to the back garden where it replaced a *Styrax japonica* that had grown too large. The coveted corner spot will now go to a weeping willow-leafed pear whose silver foliage tones beautifully with the colour of the house behind; and the pear, in its turn, will make room for a Japanese maple, unless Brenda discovers another fine small tree that appeals to her more.

More often, the introduction of a newcomer requires a farewell to something else, and Brenda's friends are beginning to look forward to the moment each spring when she will fall head over heels for a brilliant new specimen and so need to find a home for another exile.

In spite of her preference for shrubs and perennials, however, Brenda always finds some room for annuals, particularly fragrant old sweet peas. A special trellis is reserved for them, and Brenda has been known to host a midsummer garden party to which friends bring bunches of these Victorian favourites snipped from their own gardens. "This is *not* the horticultural event of the year," she says. "It's really just an excuse to drink gin." And for an afternoon at least, the serious collector and cataloguer abandons her permanent collection to acknowledge the ephemeral treasures of a single season, and indulge in the fun of the Grand Prix de Sweet Pea. ❧

TERRI WHITE AND BOB ALLEN'S GARDEN

"We overplant. We can't help ourselves."

*T*HE PRETTY HOUSE SITS ON ITS corner lot in West Point Grey in a blaze of summer glory. A neighbour, carrying his weekend shopping, pauses on the sidewalk to admire the sight. "Isn't it wonderful," he says. "It's like this all year round." His response is commonplace for the three people who live here and tend the garden as a cooperative project. They have had strangers knocking on the door to ask the name of the pink double-flowered hibiscus that blooms on the boulevard, or the purple *Clematis jackmanii* that spirals up to the eaves of the front porch each year, or the variety of petunia that cascades out of a hanging basket by the steps to the front door.

The baskets are planted each year by Terri White, who shares the main floor of the house with her husband, Colin Garnett, but many of the shrubs date from the years when the house was owned by Kitty Murdoch

and her sister. Kitty's presence is still strong in the garden that she tended for close to 40 years: forget-me-nots, bellflowers and Welsh poppies that come up all over the garden are reminders of Kitty's gardening days and the plastic animals that skulk among the foliage are her contributions too. Some people turn up their noses at the wide-eyed rabbit, the faded pheasant, the crouching squirrel, but the owners have no plans to remove them. "We didn't buy them, we're not responsible for them," says Terri. "They just are."

The third member of the trio, Bob Allen, who occupies the upper floor, used to rent his space from the Murdoch spinsters and likes the reminders of Kitty's hand in the landscaping: the mauve rhododendron that flowers in late January, the tall 'Queen Elizabeth' rose whose flowers can be picked from the front porch, the

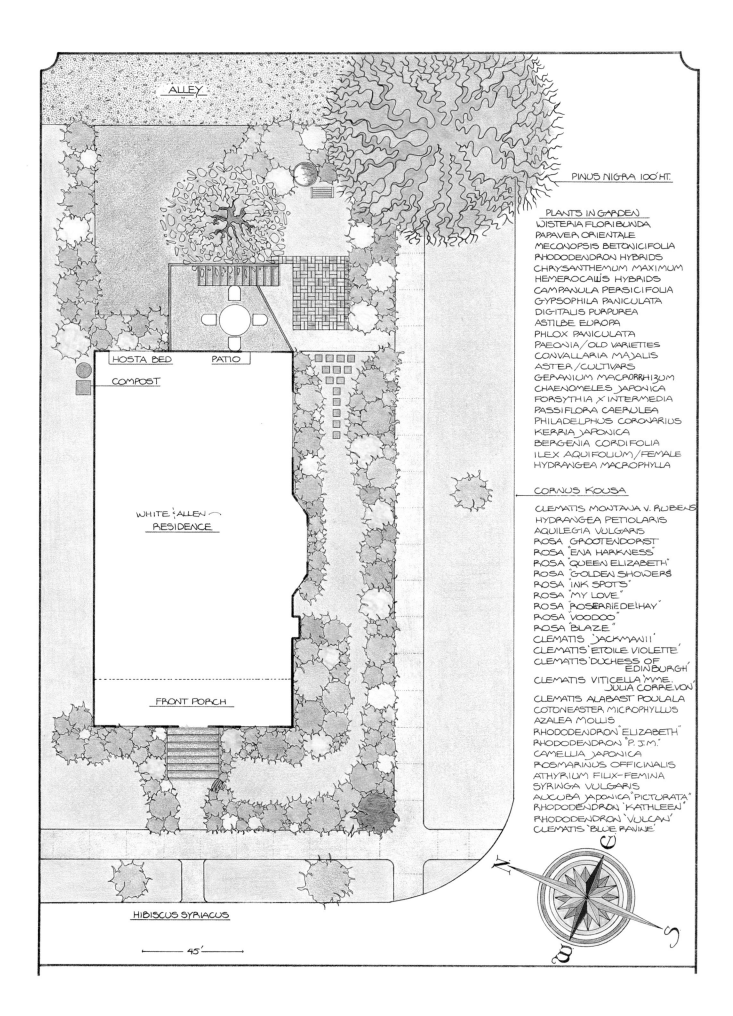

ALLEY

PINUS NIGRA 100' HT.

PLANTS IN GARDEN
WISTERIA FLORIBUNDA
PAPAVER ORIENTALE
MECONOPSIS BETONICIFOLIA
RHODODENDRON HYBRIDS
CHRYSANTHEMUM MAXIMUM
HEMEROCALLIS HYBRIDS
CAMPANULA PERSICIFOLIA
GYPSOPHILA PANICULATA
DIGITALIS PURPUREA
ASTILBE EUROPA
PHLOX PANICULATA
PAEONIA/OLD VARIETIES
CONVALLARIA MAJALIS
ASTER/CULTIVARS
GERANIUM MACRORRHIZUM
CHAENOMELES JAPONICA
FORSYTHIA X INTERMEDIA
PASSIFLORA CAERULEA
PHILADELPHUS CORONARIUS
KERRIA JAPONICA
BERGENIA CORDIFOLIA
ILEX AQUIFOLIUM/FEMALE
HYDRANGEA MACROPHYLLA

CORNUS KOUSA

CLEMATIS MONTANA V. RUBENS
HYDRANGEA PETIOLARIS
AQUILEGIA VULGARIS
ROSA GROOTENDORST
ROSA "ENA HARKNESS"
ROSA "QUEEN ELIZABETH"
ROSA "GOLDEN SHOWERS"
ROSA "INK SPOTS"
ROSA "MY LOVE"
ROSA "ROSERAIE DE L'HAY"
ROSA "VOODOO"
ROSA "BLAZE"
CLEMATIS "JACKMANII"
CLEMATIS "ETOILE VIOLETTE"
CLEMATIS "DUCHESS OF
        EDINBURGH"
CLEMATIS VITICELLA "MME.
        JULIA CORREVON"
CLEMATIS ALABAST POULALA
COTONEASTER MICROPHYLLUS
AZALEA MOLLIS
RHODODENDRON "ELIZABETH"
RHODODENDRON "P.J.M."
CAMELLIA JAPONICA
ROSMARINUS OFFICINALIS
ATHYRIUM FILIX-FEMINA
SYRINGA VULGARIS
AUCUBA JAPONICA "PICTURATA"
RHODODENDRON "KATHLEEN"
RHODODENDRON "VULCAN"
CLEMATIS "BLUE RAVINE"

HOSTA BED   PATIO

COMPOST

WHITE : ALLEN
RESIDENCE

FRONT PORCH

HIBISCUS SYRIACUS

⊢——— 45' ———⊣

N

E

S

W

soft orange daylily by the sidewalk, as well as the quirky animals.

Kitty was fond of roses and 'Queen Elizabeth' shares the garden with a huge crimson rugosa rose, 'F. J. Groot-endorst', on the corner, and several vigorous climbers on the side fence, as well as a deep pink shrub rose that blooms from late spring to first frost, making a fragrant hedge along the front of the house. The climber 'Golden Showers' scales the north side of the front porch, and Bob's liking for symmetry has led to a matching one on the south side. Both men have reservations about Terri's interplanting of these beds with annual *Cosmos*, but all agree on the beauty of rhododendron 'Kathleen', planted, of course, by the late Kitty, which graces the front path and is a traffic-stopper when covered with its peach-pink blossoms. It is one of the few plants that Terri conscientiously deadheads because she hates to see it looking bedraggled. Nearby, another rhododendron, the brilliant red 'Vulcan', backs up against the house, crowding a red-flowered camellia into the corner formed by the front stairs. Above them, planters spill a colourful stream of lobelia, solanum, fuchsias and petunias in summer, replaced in winter by a more sober arrangement of pansies and ivy. A pot of lavender sits by the front door, and tomatoes thrive in the shelter of the porch overhang.

Along the side of the house, a white wisteria scrambles up the chimney to the eaves, where it wraps protective tendrils around a bird's nest. All three owners are bird lovers, and conversation is diverted from the garden by the sight of an eagle flying from behind the giant black pine that dominates the south sidewalk. Colin has hung an old cherry tree in the small back garden with birdhouses whose patrons may have attracted the eagle. The birds in their turn had a field day with the first occupants of a ladybug box that he installed in a sweep of passionflower vine under one of the bay windows.

Vines are another feature of this garden, particularly clematis. The railing of the small back deck is invisible under a cloak of *Clematis montana* var. *rubens,* and *C.* 'Blue Ravine' twines up the trunk of the cherry. 'Madame Julia Correvon' fights with a rose for fence space and 'Autumn Splendour' is literally setting out to tangle with the wisteria. On a simple trellis anchored to the south wall, sweet peas sway in summer breezes.

Under these successive curtains of colour, the beds that run the long south border of the property begin the year with blue and pink spikes of lungwort and ivory bells of lily-of-the-valley, followed by peonies, hardy geraniums and the silky orange flowers of oriental poppies blotched with deepest purple. In midsummer, a forest of tall phlox springs up to engulf the black-painted metal fence in sheets of bright pink, purple and white. By this time, the roses and the midseason clematis are in bloom, the baskets, pots and planters are at their peak, and people are stopping in their tracks to admire the show. The three owners are modest about the attention they attract. "Kitty started it," they say. "We just carried on." ❧

PAGE 86
Clematis jackmanii scrambles up the front porch toward a basket of petunias. Rose 'Queen Elizabeth' adds a touch of pink.

PAGE 87
Ornamental cabbages 'Red Pigeon' and 'White Pigeon' provide autumn colour.

PAGE 89
A white wisteria climbs to the eaves of the Craftsman-style cottage. Tall crimson rose 'F. J. Grootendorst' fills a corner of the garden.

PAGE 90–91
The front porch is festooned with hanging baskets and boxes of bright annuals.

SIDNEY SHADBOLT'S GARDEN

"I just plant what anybody gives me and if I don't like it, I give it to somebody else."

On Vancouver's east side, just north of Kingsway, a few of the early streets diverge from the city grid, following instead the diagonal line of Kingsway itself. The street that Sidney Shadbolt lives on aligns with the grid but her house, the original farmhouse of the area, sits skewed on the lot, parallel to Kingsway and presents its faded yellow clapboard side to the street from behind a screen of rough-barked black locust trees *(Robinia pseudoacacia)*. From the high third storey a broad verandah still commands an imposing view toward the North Shore mountains.

Little is visible from the street except the garage doors, a bank of rhododendrons along the sidewalk and a huge wall of laurel hedge that hugs the north boundary. Indeed, these seem to fill the available space. Yet within the angle they form with the house, there is room for a neat, paved courtyard, its geometry a contrast to their sombre bulk. Tall stands of bamboo flank a flight of stairs and a fountain of *Leycesteria formosa* dangles its curious beads of black and burgundy over the path to a wooden bench. Underfoot, pots of tangerine impatiens make bright splashes of colour among the greens of ferns and hostas, while overhead layers of leaves from the spreading branches of witch hazels ascend towards the high filigree of the black locust trees. Great ropes of ivy have slung themselves around the largest craggy trunk beside the bench, bursting into leaf as they reach the brighter light above. A purple-leafed plum tree is swathed in veils of clematis and the pillars that hold up the entry porch to the main floor of the house are thick with ivy and spirals of honeysuckle. In this small space there seems to be twice as much garden layered in the air as on the ground.

Because of the odd angle of the house to its lot, it sits

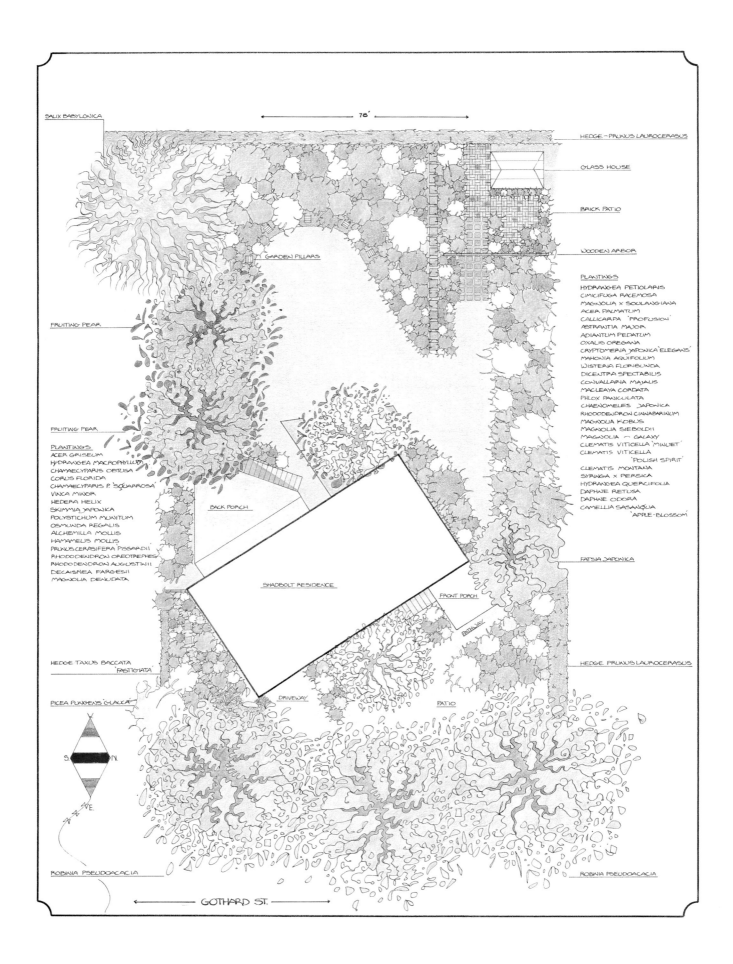

SALIX BABYLONICA

78'

HEDGE ~ PRUNUS LAUROCERASUS

GLASS HOUSE

BRICK PATIO

GARDEN PILLARS

WOODEN ARBOR

FRUITING PEAR

PLANTINGS
HYDRANGEA PETIOLARIS
CIMICIFUGA RACEMOSA
MAGNOLIA X SOULANGIANA
ACER PALMATUM
CALLICARPA 'PROFUSION'
ASTRANTIA MAJOR
ADIANTUM PEDATUM
OXALIS OREGANA
CRYPTOMERIA JAPONICA 'ELEGANS'
MAHONIA AQUIFOLIUM
WISTERIA FLORIBUNDA
DICENTRA SPECTABILIS
CONVALLARIA MAJALIS
MACLEAYA CORDATA
PHLOX PANICULATA
CHAENOMELES JAPONICA
RHODODENDRON CINNABARINUM
MAGNOLIA KOBUS
MAGNOLIA SIEBOLDII
MAGNOLIA ~ GALAXY
CLEMATIS VITICELLA 'MINUET'
CLEMATIS VITICELLA
          'POLISH SPIRIT'
CLEMATIS MONTANA
SYRINGA X PERSICA
HYDRANGEA QUERCIFOLIA
DAPHNE RETUSA
DAPHNE ODORA
CAMELLIA SASANQUA
          'APPLE-BLOSSOM'

FRUITING PEAR

PLANTINGS
ACER GRISEUM
HYDRANGEA MACROPHYLLUM
CHAMAECYPARIS OBTUSA
CORUS FLORIDA
CHAMAECYPARIS P. 'SQUARROSA'
VINCA MINOR
HEDERA HELIX
SKIMMIA JAPONICA
POLYSTICHUM MUNITUM
OSMUNDA REGALIS
ALCHEMILLA MOLLIS
HAMAMELIS MOLLIS
PRUNUS CERASIFERA PISSARDII
RHODODENDRON ONEOTREPHES
RHODODENDRON AUGUSTINII
DECAISNEA FARGESII
MAGNOLIA DENUDATA

BACK PORCH

FATSIA JAPONICA

SHADBOLT RESIDENCE

FRONT PORCH

PATHWAY

HEDGE TAXUS BACCATA
          'FASTIGIATA'

HEDGE PRUNUS LAUROCERASUS

PICEA PUNGENS 'GLAUCA'

DRIVEWAY

PATIO

ROBINIA PSEUDOACACIA

ROBINIA PSEUDOACACIA

GOTHARD ST.

"This garden looks really casual, but in fact it's planned very carefully."

tight against its southern boundary, allowing a much wider stretch of ground than normal on the north side. The path into this area leads under a ceiling of *Fatsia japonica* foliage to where a white iron gate defines the halfway point between shade and sunlight. Here the surface underfoot changes from rounded pebbles to springy grass printed with shadows from the *Fatsia* and a fine-leafed Japanese maple against the house. As the space widens, the grass floods out into a pool of smooth green lawn.

On a small, stone-flagged patio where she has a table and a couple of chairs, Sidney Shadbolt watches over the changing face of her broad and varied garden, the whole enclosed by high laurel hedges and board fencing. Pots of flowers and a stone birdbath and fountain clutter the space around her.

Back here, the width of the double lot has allowed her to divide the garden into several areas, each slightly screened from the others by tall shrubs. Dominating the scene is a semicircle of tall white columns which stands pristine and unadorned around the far edge of the lawn. When the Shadbolts arrived twenty years ago, they found some of the columns lying in the grass while a few still supported a rickety porch. Now rescued and carefully placed around the arc of lawn, they add a classical air to the garden, enhanced by a weeping willow that softens the composition with streamers of gold-green leaves. In the dappled light of late afternoon sun on this green stage, a ballerina from Swan Lake would not be out of place. More practically, the Shadbolts often use the lawn in summer for games of bocce and croquet with their friends, many of whom have become Sidney Shadbolt's "dedicated slaves," contributing plants and pruning skills to the garden.

Behind the white columns, a border of phlox — "the backbone of the garden"— springs up each year against the backdrop of laurel hedge. An old apple tree, lurking behind the willow fronds, yields buckets of apples every year while managing to ward off the advances of a persistent wisteria which has already brought down another apple and now engulfs the old trunk. Below the phlox, iris and peonies flourish among clumps of fleshy sea-green *Sedum spectabile* and the silver-spotted leaves of Italian arum. Sunflowers screen a raspberry patch with a tangle of herbs swirling around the canes. Garlic has escaped from its original location and is everywhere in the garden, tying the disparate areas together with its stout green stems and starry flowers.

Where the curve of flower bed ends its loop around the lawn, a path branches off behind a tree peony to still more garden. Now the surface becomes chunky old brick with volunteer forget-me-nots and foxgloves sprouting from the cracks. A small greenhouse appears beyond a trellis of wide-spaced lath embroidered with wisps of yellow nasturtium. One end of the trellis buts up against a solid post supporting three birdhouses, which cluster at the top like a modern townhouse complex. Just visible beyond them is the lavender blue of the mountains.

Pots of various sizes and shapes fill odd corners, brimming with everything from sage to hibiscus to zinnias. The largest containers hold tender shrubs such as purple *Tibouchina urvilleana* and trumpet-flowered *Brugmansia*, which contribute their exotic colour and fragrance to the garden in the warmth of summer and can be moved into shelter when the season changes. There is even a *Cereus,* which blooms for just one night of the year. "You wake up and smell this wonderful fragrance," Sidney Shadbolt says, "as it unfolds before your eyes."

The greenhouse nurtures flats of annual seedlings in spring, an eclectic mix of cosmos, sweet peas, cleome, heliotrope and all kinds of daisies, including a vigorous strain of marigolds from seed that Sidney brought back from a trip to Kiev. The smaller plants go into all the containers while the larger ones are scattered among the perennials, giving the garden an air of abundance late into the year.

On a warm afternoon in early fall, when leaves and flowers are just beginning to droop and wither, the air is redolent with the smell of wine emanating from the neighbour's rampant grapevine drooping over the fence and alive with the brisk flutter of chickadees and jays as they come and go among the dishevelled heads of sunflowers. Alstroemeria and Michaelmas daisies lean among the sunflower stalks and the slate blue foliage of *Romneya coulteri* froths between them. A magnolia on the west side of the garden doubles the strength of sunlight with its filter of golden leaves and a dazzled lady bug alights on Sidney Shadbolt's cheek, a good omen for the season's end. ☙

PAGE 92
Wisteria and a weeping willow make a classical composition with white columns around the lawn.

PAGE 93
Rhododendrons and bamboo screen the old farmhouse from the street.

PAGE 95
A white Exbury azalea is underplanted with clumps of blue Aquilegia and yellow leopard's bane (*Doronicum plantagineum*).

PAGE 97 ABOVE
Two-toned orange bells of *Rhododendron cinnabarinum* lean across the grass toward blue iris and a Japanese maple.

PAGE 97 BELOW
Sword ferns, rhododendrons and witch hazels surround a simple seat.

LINDA FOX'S GARDEN

"When I got into gardening, it was with the intent of having a winter garden. Winter can be long here, and I wanted something green and living to look at."

Small, east side properties are rarely landscaped with as many imposing trees as Linda and Peter Fox's garden. Even on a hot summer afternoon, it is cool and green, thanks to the varying degrees of shade cast by a Douglas fir and a deodar cedar in the square of backyard garden, plus another deodar with a couple of young spruce and two purple-leafed plums, remnants of the city landscaping, on the south-facing boulevard. Around the corner, the west wall of the house faces a tall oak wedged into the tiny front yard, competing for size with a horse chestnut on the sidewalk. A katsura tree and a purple smokebush anchor the curve of the corner.

Under this lofty canopy, the Foxes have paved, planted and potted to create an atmosphere of deep woods privacy which envelops their house in its own magic circle. Coming upon their leafy corner is more like coming upon Snow White's dwelling in the forest than arriving at a typical suburban intersection. This is partly due to the fact that the original strip of parched grass between sidewalk and road is now a series of neat rectangular beds, contained by turkey-red edging bricks and separated by square pavers in the same muted hue. Within the beds, an eclectic mix of heathers, hostas, low-growing azaleas and a multitude of different sedums defy the extremes of dappled to dense shade and harsh summer sun, and provide a touch of colour in their different flowering seasons. In summer, Linda interplants with a scattering of begonias and impatiens for additional colour accents; in winter, black-faced pansies fill the gaps.

Taller plants occupy the long, narrow bed that runs under the windows of the house, blending their greens and browns with the mahogany stain on the shingles

BACKYARD PLANTING
HYDRANGEA ASPERA
THALICTRUM AQUILEGIFOLIUM "HEWITTS DOUBLE"
COTINUS COGGYGRIA "ROYAL PURPLE"
FAGUS SYLVATICA "ATROPURPUREA"
ACER PALMATUM "DISSECTUM VIRIDIS"
DICENTRA SPECTABILIS "ALBA"
CORYLUS AVELLANA "CONTORTA"
CARAGANA ARBORESCENS "PENDULA"
ENKIANTHUS CAMPANULATUS "RED BELLS"
RHODODENRON "PRESIDENT ROOSEVELT"
CLEMATIS "ROUGE CARDINAL"

CLEMATIS ARMANDII
PINUS SYLVESTRIS
PRIMULA V. "APRIL ROSE"
BLECHNUM SPICANT
ADIANTUM PEDATUM
OSMUNDA REGALIS
HEDRA HELIX
ROSA "EASY LIVIN"
PIERIS JAPONICA
PHOTINIA FRASERI
CLEMATIS "THE PRESIDENT"

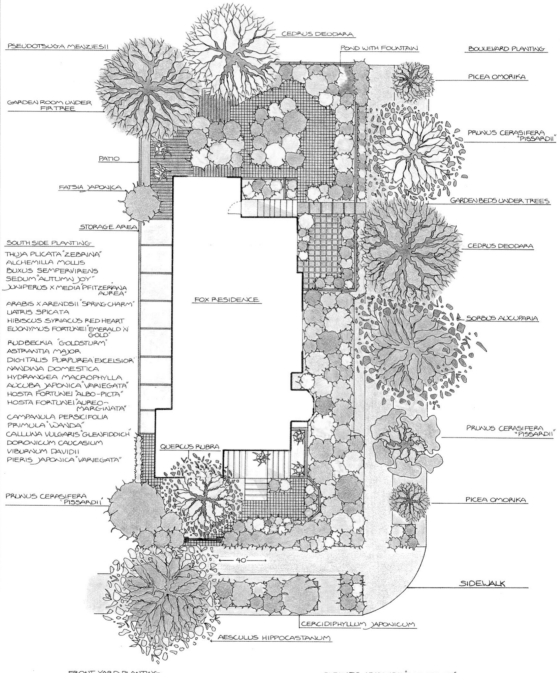

PSEUDOTSUGA MENZIESII

CEDRUS DEODARA

POND WITH FOUNTAIN

BOULEVARD PLANTING

PICEA OMORIKA

GARDEN ROOM UNDER
FIR TREE

PRUNUS CERASIFERA
"PISSARDII"

PATIO

FATSIA JAPONICA

GARDEN BEDS UNDER TREES

STORAGE AREA

CEDRUS DEODARA

SOUTH SIDE PLANTING
THUJA PLICATA "ZEBRINA"
ALCHEMILLA MOLLIS
BUXUS SEMPERVIRENS
SEDUM "AUTUMN JOY"
JUNIPERUS X MEDIA "PFITZERIANA
AUREA"
ARABIS X ARENDSII "SPRING CHARM"
LIATRIS SPICATA
HIBISCUS SYRIACUS "RED HEART"
EUONYMUS FORTUNEI "EMERALD 'N'
GOLD"
RUDBECKIA "GOLDSTURM"
ASTRANTIA MAJOR
DIGITALIS PURPUREA "EXCELSIOR"
NANDINA DOMESTICA
HYDRANGEA MACROPHYLLA
AUCUBA JAPONICA "VARIEGATA"
HOSTA FORTUNEI "ALBO-PICTA"
HOSTA FORTUNEI "AUREO-
MARGINATA"
CAMPANULA PERSICIFOLIA
PRIMULA "WANDA"
CALLUNA VULGARIS "GLENFIDDICH"
DORONICUM CAUCASIUM
VIBURNUM DAVIDII
PIERIS JAPONICA "VARIEGATA"

FOX RESIDENCE

SORBUS AUCUPARIA

QUERCUS RUBRA

PRUNUS CERASIFERA
"PISSARDII"

PRUNUS CERASIFERA
"PISSARDII"

PICEA OMORIKA

40'

SIDEWALK

CERCIDIPHYLLUM JAPONICUM

AESCULUS HIPPOCASTANUM

FRONT YARD PLANTING
CEDRUS ATLANTICA "GLAUCA"
PIERIS JAPONICA
VINCA MINOR "VARIEGATA"
GALIUM ODORATUM
HEDGE-THUJA OCCIDENTALIS "FASTIGIATA"
ADIANTUM PEDATUM
JUNIPERUS SQUAMATA "BLUE STAR"
CHAMAECYPARIS OBTUSA "CORALLIFORMIS"
CHAMAECYPARIS PISIFERA "FILIFERA AUREA"

CLEMATIS ARMANDII "SNOWDRIFT"
CAMELLIA JAPONICA
ACER PALMATUM
VIBURNUM PLICATUM "SUMMER SNOWFLAKE"
PARTHENOCISSUS TRICUSPIDATA
EUPHORBIA DULCIS "CHAMAELEON"
HEDERA HELIX "ITTSY BITTSY"
RHODODENDRON HYBRIDS
DRYOPTERIS ERYTHROSORA
HEDERA COLCHICA "DENTATA" VARIEGATA

and the sea-green of the window casings. The bluish tones in the fleshy leaves of *Sedum* 'Autumn Joy' exactly match the colour of the trim, while the fern-like foliage of *Pieris japonica* and *Nandina domestica* adds a richer green in summer and bursts into flame as fall approaches. The patent-leather leaves of camellias contribute the darkest, shiniest green of all, and a wash of soft pastel flowers in early spring. Stiff blades of *Crocosmia* 'Lucifer' assert their independence in colour, shape and texture from the hydrangea behind, even before they sprout arching stems of cardinal-red

flowers. A variegated *Aucuba*, hunched against the wall, echoes the dappled sunlight in the green and pale gold pattern of its leaves.

This is the shared part of the garden, a gift to their neighbours as much as for their own enjoyment. Behind a latticed fence festooned with clematis is their private domain, a courtyard paved in small square bricks and crammed with pots of every size and shape. Confining plants to containers allows Linda Fox to move them around and change them as the seasons change without interfering with the pockets of permanent planting that constitute an evergreen backdrop. Here, as elsewhere, foliage predominates, with colour provided by the subtle shadings of silver and plum in the fronds of Japanese painted fern or the bold lime, purple and canary yellow of *Coleus* leaves.

In one corner, water bubbles over a stone umbrella sheltering two huddled children and drips into a minuscule pond. Behind this bit of whimsy, two long, horizontal bands of mirror at eye-level create the illusion of a more distant garden glimpsed through gaps in the fence.

Across the courtyard, raised slightly on a dais of wooden slats, is the outdoor room from which the Foxes can contemplate this scene. It is an outdoor room in a most literal and unusual sense—a 1940s stage-set in miniature, dominated by a fireplace complete with simulated glowing coals, a mantel and a mirror. An elaborate fretwork of turned wooden spindles, which began life as a Mexican bed frame, encloses either side, making a space just large enough for two chairs and a simple table. Suitably retro ornaments, many doing double duty as candle holders, fill the mantel, prints of angelic Victorian children hang on the "walls," and a chandelier dangles above. The effect is slightly surreal, as if the Mad Hatter's tea party has appeared from a rabbit-hole in the back yard of this ivy-garlanded Vancouver garden.

Adventurous as she is in adding such startling elements to the garden, Linda prefers not to experiment when it comes to plants. She favours the dependability of foliage over the more fleeting and unpredictable habits of flowers. Tidy, compact growth which "doesn't get leggy or need staking" characterizes her favourite plants, and paving, which can be swept of falling leaves and petals, is less demanding and easier to maintain than grass. Linda can often be found, broom in hand, keeping the sidewalk free of debris—maintaining a garden for which the word "neat" is appropriate in more than one sense. ᴄˁ

PAGE 98
Begonias, impatiens and threadleaf cypress (*Chamaecyparis pisifera* 'Filifera Aurea') occupy a cluster of pots.

PAGE 99
Beside a *Pieris japonica* an oriental pot holds plants in matching hues.

PAGE 101
A study in green.

PAGE 102–3
Pink leaves of *Acer palmatum* overhang a clump of maidenhair ferns

PAGE 103 RIGHT
Ivy surrounds the outdoor room.

AUDREY LITHERLAND'S GARDEN

"When I started it was like a battle field and I just put everything in. Now it's a case of taking things out, they've grown so much."

BELOW THE ESCARPMENT LINED WITH the mansions of Southwest Marine Drive, the Fraser River flats stretch to the western horizon in a peaceful landscape of parks and golf courses. The small plot that Audrey Litherland gardens in a well-groomed subdivision of cedar-shingled townhouses overlooks this green and pleasant playground and borrows some of its features for its own enhancement.

The manicured turf and a glittering thread of water which can be seen between the trunks of a row of lofty poplars provide a frame for the flower-filled patio. Here the Litherlands spend much of the warm, summer weather at ease on the cushions of their comfortable cane chairs. Quarry tiles make a practical floor for this outdoor room, and a canopy protects it from the glare of afternoon sun. Where the tiles end, waves of surfinias, heliotrope, bacopa and other annuals ripple out from long, narrow beds across the smooth surface. Beyond them, the ground steps up a level onto a terrace of wooden slats bounded by a low wall of planters in the same material. Clematis and ivy overflow from the top of the wall so vigorously that the bench seats set into it are too festooned with tendrils of foliage to allow for sitting down. At the centre, a rustic gate, overhung by an arch thick with ivy, jasmine and clematis, frames a large shrub of *Lavatera* 'Barnsley' covered in fragile, satin-pink flowers.

Private property ends here where the land drops down abruptly to river level, but Audrey has filled the right of way between her gate and the golf course with a

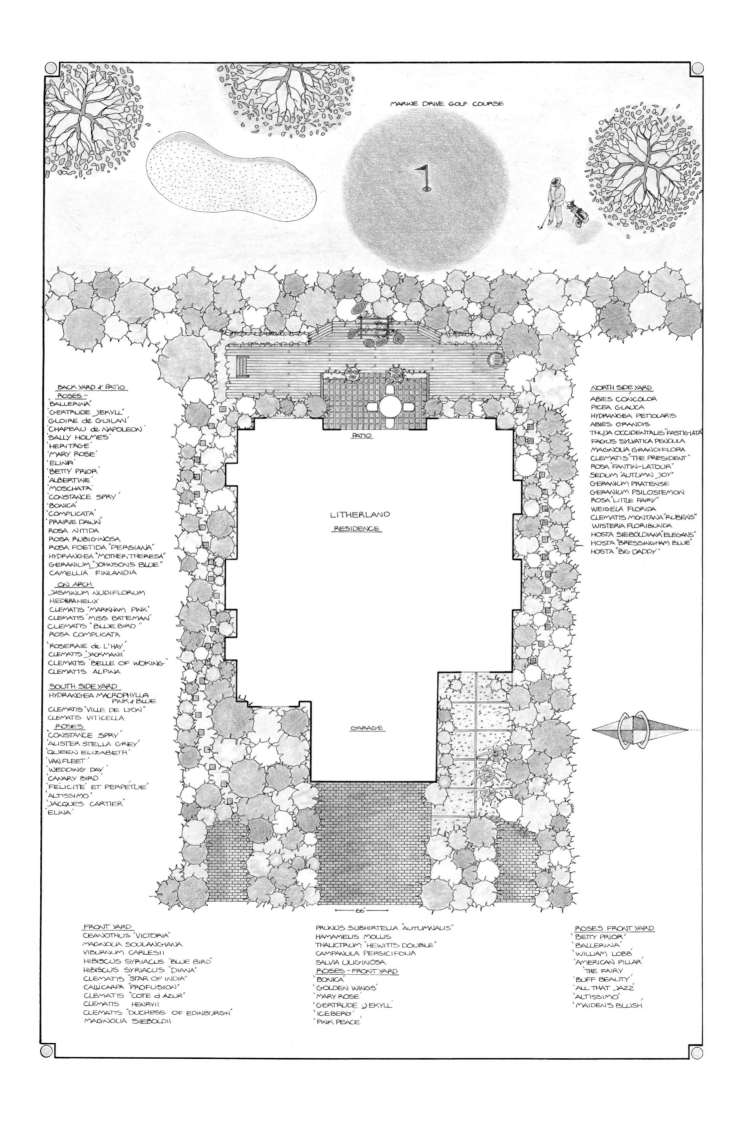

MARINE DRIVE GOLF COURSE

LITHERLAND RESIDENCE

PATIO

GARAGE

BACK YARD & PATIO
ROSES -
'BALLERINA'
'GERTRUDE JEKYLL'
'GLOIRE de GUILAN'
'CHAPEAU de NAPOLEON'
'SALLY HOLMES'
'HERITAGE'
'MARY ROSE'
'ELINA'
'BETTY PRIOR'
'ALBERTINE'
'MOSCHATA'
'CONSTANCE SPRY'
'BONICA'
'COMPLICATA'
'PRAIRIE DAWN'
ROSA NITIDA
ROSA RUBIGINOSA
ROSA FOETIDA 'PERSIANA'
HYDRANGEA 'MOTHER THERESA'
GERANIUM 'JOHNSON'S BLUE'
CAMELLIA FINLANDIA

ON ARCH
JASMINUM NUDIFLORUM
HEDERA HELIX
CLEMATIS 'MARKHAM PINK'
CLEMATIS 'MISS BATEMAN'
CLEMATIS 'BLUE BIRD'
ROSA COMPLICATA

'ROSERAIE de L'HAY'
CLEMATIS 'JACKMANII'
CLEMATIS 'BELLE OF WOKING'
CLEMATIS ALPINA

SOUTH SIDE YARD
HYDRANGEA MACROPHYLLA
                PINK & BLUE
CLEMATIS 'VILLE DE LYON'
CLEMATIS VITICELLA
ROSES -
'CONSTANCE SPRY'
'ALISTER STELLA GREY'
'QUEEN ELIZABETH'
'VAN FLEET'
'WEDDING DAY'
'CANARY BIRD'
'FELICITE ET PERPETUE'
'ALTISSIMO'
'JACQUES CARTIER'
'ELINA'

NORTH SIDE YARD
ABIES CONCOLOR
PICEA GLAUCA
HYDRANGEA PETIOLARIS
ABIES GRANDIS
THUJA OCCIDENTALIS FASTIGIATA
FAGUS SYLVATICA PENDULA
MAGNOLIA GRANDIFLORA
CLEMATIS 'THE PRESIDENT'
ROSA FANTIN-LATOUR
SEDUM 'AUTUMN JOY'
GERANIUM PRATENSE
GERANIUM PSILOSTEMON
ROSA 'LITTLE FAIRY'
WEIGELA FLORIDA
CLEMATIS MONTANA 'RUBENS'
WISTERIA FLORIBUNDA
HOSTA SIEBOLDIANA 'ELEGANS'
HOSTA 'BRESSINGHAM BLUE'
HOSTA 'BIG DADDY'

FRONT YARD
CEANOTHUS 'VICTORIA'
MAGNOLIA SOULANGIANA
VIBURNUM CARLESII
HIBISCUS SYRIACUS 'BLUE BIRD'
HIBISCUS SYRIACUS 'DIANA'
CLEMATIS 'STAR OF INDIA'
CALLICARPA 'PROFUSION'
CLEMATIS 'COTE d'AZUR'
CLEMATIS HENRYII
CLEMATIS 'DUCHESS OF EDINBURGH'
MAGNOLIA SIEBOLDII

PRUNUS SUBHIRTELLA 'AUTUMNALIS'
HAMAMELIS MOLLIS
THALICTRUM 'HEWITT'S DOUBLE'
CAMPANULA PERSICIFOLIA
SALVIA ULIGINOSA
ROSES - FRONT YARD
'BONICA'
'GOLDEN WINGS'
'MARY ROSE'
'GERTRUDE JEKYLL'
'ICEBERG'
'PINK PEACE'

ROSES FRONT YARD
'BETTY PRIOR'
'BALLERINA'
'WILLIAM LOBB'
'AMERICAN PILLAR'
'THE FAIRY'
'BUFF BEAUTY'
'ALL THAT JAZZ'
'ALTISSIMO'
'MAIDEN'S BLUSH'

66'

swath of prickly rugosa roses and other well-armed shrubs to deter the coyotes which have taken up residence along the shore. Roses are a recurring element throughout the garden and many different varieties are interspersed among the profusion of perennials and vines. A pair of standards of 'The Fairy', dotted with small pink rosettes, flank the step leading up from patio to deck. The crisp green leaves of an old gallica, 'Complicata,' soften the outline of the west wall, brightening it in summer with large crimson flowers and in autumn with rich red hips. The thornless stems of a true musk rose, *Rosa moschata*, twine above the windows, while a bevy of pink 'Bonica' roses fills out the boxes underneath.

Among the tall plants that loom above the narrow path around the southern end of the house are vigorous climbing roses like 'Altissimo' with blood-red single flowers, blowsy pink 'Constance Spry' and venerable 'Zéphirine Drouhin' whose bold purple flowers have a powerful perfume. They jostle for elbow room with lusty plants of *Hibiscus syriacus* and *Viburnum plicatum,* a lilac and a magnolia, all underplanted with waist-high clumps of phlox and perennial lobelias in shades of pink and white.

On the opposite side of the house, an equally narrow space is filled to overflowing with shade-loving hostas and hardy geraniums, hydrangeas and rhododendrons with a backdrop of hummingbird vine (*Campsis* × *tagliabuana*) whose orange trumpets only bloom on the other side of the fence, giving more pleasure to Audrey's neighbour than to herself.

Even along the road frontage, largely occupied by the garage and its necessary access, Audrey has managed to cram in a generous assortment of plants, creating both height and profusion by raising the beds in staggered pyramids. The blue flowers of *Salvia uliginosa* wave from the top of one mound, surrounded by white 'Casablanca' lilies, the cerise and black flowers of *Gera-*

nium psilostemon, and roses like pale pink 'Fantin Latour' and soft yellow 'Elina' interlaced with clematis.

On the other side of the driveway, towering canes of Meidiland roses arch over smaller roses. 'The Fairy' appears again in a prominent role here, largely, Audrey admits, because she acquired a bulk lot of this particular plant at a nursery sale.

Surveying the rampant growth, Audrey is amazed by how everything has grown. "When I started," she recalls, "it was like a battlefield and I just put everything in. Now it's a case of taking things out, they've grown so much."

In fact, it's a challenge to find and follow the path to the front door—like finding the gap in the curtain on a theatre stage. Here the curtain is woven of dark fronds of foliage and tendrils of vine, punctuated by shots of colour: a white *Hibiscus syriacus* 'Diana' and a tall white *Brugmansia* in a terracotta pot; the tiny lavender bells of *Thalictrum* 'Hewitt's Double', a scattering of peach-leaved campanulas and a row of fragrant annuals like heliotrope and night-scented stock in an assortment of containers crowding right up to the doorstep.

Throughout the garden, there is a sense of enclosure, a slightly dream-like quality, luxuriant, benign. Perhaps it is that the paving underfoot, the gaily coloured tapestry of annuals, perennials and flowering shrubs, the overflowing, random planting controlled and confined by a strict geometry of design, and the distant scene of broad, emerald green river flats and waving poplars has little to do with the brooding coniferous forests and rugged mountain peaks of Vancouver's indigenous landscape. Nor is it, however, representative of the English influence that tames tall cedars and jagged Douglas firs with a foreground of broad, curving border and rolling lawn. It has echoes of the symmetry of French and Italian gardens, and the idyllic landscapes of children's books— like a world in a glass paperweight, serenely oblivious to the harsher territory outside its confines. ❧

PAGE 104
Ivy, roses, jasmine and clematis cover an arch.

PAGE 105
Leaves of a young *Brugmansia versicolor* frame a birdbath.

PAGE 107
Hydrangeas in the side passage.

PAGE 109 TOP
Comfy seats on the patio are shaded by rose 'The Fairy' and *Hydrangea* 'Soeur Thérèse'.

PAGE 109 BELOW
Pots of *Brugmansia versicolor* flank the path to the front door.

ANDRE CHEVRIER AND DONNA DAVIS'S GARDEN

"We used to have long conversations as to what the garden should be, but in the end we just let it evolve."

IT IS NOT SURPRISING THAT THE narrow strip of earth outside the fence-line of the small lot where André Chevrier and Donna Davis live has been co-opted as part of an extended landscape. After all, a modern Kitsilano townhouse with a pocket-handkerchief garden does not immediately seem to offer much scope for enthusiastic gardeners.

What is intriguing at first glance is the desert theme the couple, both with Prairie roots, have chosen for this streetside garden. Indeed, some of the plants – sagebrush, potentillas, yuccas – have accompanied André from Saskatchewan to enhance the grey and silver theme that prevails here. Height is provided by buddleias, some windmill palms (*Trachycarpus fortunei*), a huge yucca with an undulating grey trunk, and a tamarisk whose tassels of dusky pink flowers echo the colour of the gravel that carpets the ground. Spanish lavender and *Senecio greyi* contribute more hues of silver-blue to the mix, the *Senecio* brightening the composition with its vivid yellow flowers in summer. Thin spines of a yucca and the crinkly blue foliage of a horned poppy (*Glaucium corniculatum*) enhance the desert theme. Near the gate, André has shaped the branches of a spreading rosemary to follow the outline of a large slab of sandstone. Oddly enough, the cedar hedge behind this "New Mexico" garden works very well as an unassertive green backdrop, while providing privacy for the courtyard within.

The gate to the inner sanctum, an elaborate construction of snaking metal bars, and the lush banana palm just inside signal a change in atmosphere—still suggestive of light and heat, but now more Morocco than Moose Jaw. Large pots overflowing with acid green

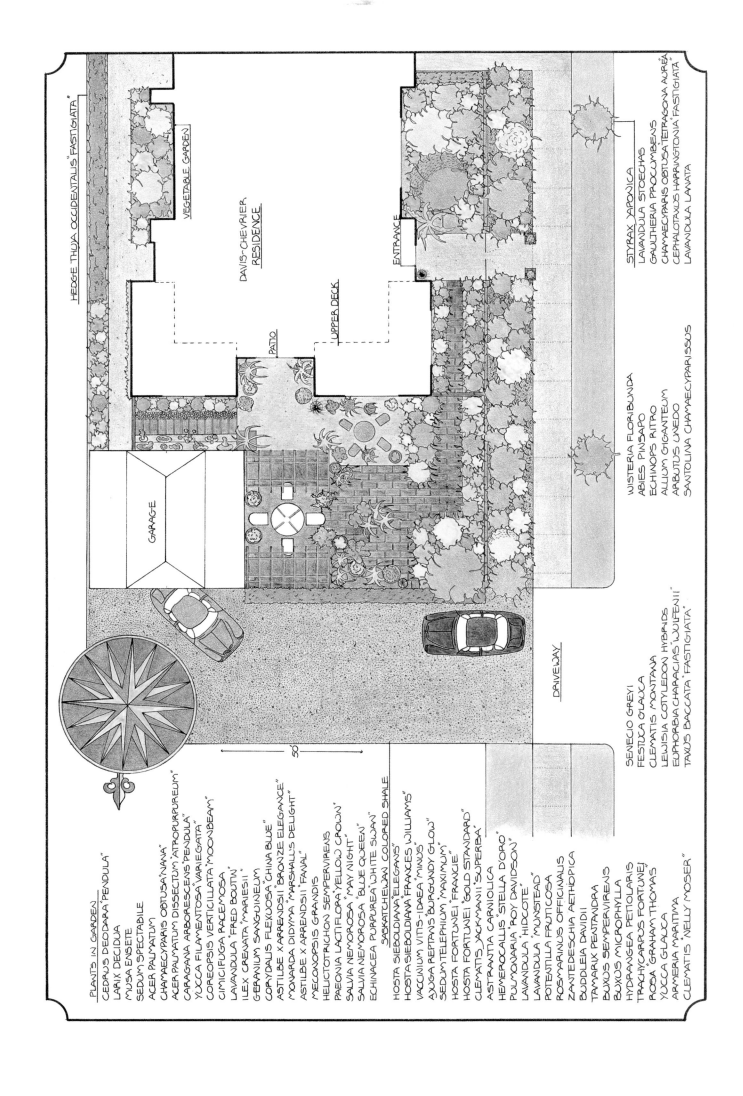

HEDGE THUJA OCCIDENTALIS "FASTIGIATA"

VEGETABLE GARDEN

DAVIS-CHEVRIER RESIDENCE

PATIO

UPPER DECK

ENTRANCE

GARAGE

50

DRIVEWAY

PLANTS IN GARDEN
CEDRUS DEODARA "PENDULA"
LARIX DECIDUA
MUSA ENSETE
SEDUM SPECTABILE
ACER PALMATUM
CHAMAECYPARIS OBTUSA "NANA"
ACER PALMATUM DISSECTUM "ATROPURPUREUM"
CARAGANA ARBORESCENS "PENDULA"
YUCCA FILAMENTOSA "VARIEGATA"
COREOPSIS VERTICILLATA "MOONBEAM"
CIMICIFUGA RACEMOSA
LAVANDULA "FRED BOUTIN"
ILEX CRENATA "MARIESII"
GERANIUM SANGUINEUM
CORYDALIS FLEXUOSA "CHINA BLUE"
ASTILBE X ARENDSII "BRONZE ELEGANCE"
MONARDA DIDYMA "MARSHALL'S DELIGHT"
ASTILBE X ARENDSII "FANAL"
MECONOPSIS GRANDIS
HELICTOTRICHON SEMPERVIRENS
PAEONIA LACTIFLORA "YELLOW CROWN"
SALVIA NEMOROSA "MAY NIGHT"
SALVIA NEMOROSA "BLUE QUEEN"
ECHINACEA PURPUREA "WHITE SWAN"
     SASKATCHEWAN COLORED SHALE
HOSTA SIEBOLDIANA "ELEGANS"
HOSTA SIEBOLDIANA "FRANCES WILLIAMS"
VACCINIUM VITIS-IDAEA "MINUS"
AJUGA REPTANS "BURGUNDY GLOW"
SEDUM TELEPHIUM "MAXIMUM"
HOSTA FORTUNEI "FRANCE"
HOSTA FORTUNEI "GOLD STANDARD"
CLEMATIS JACKMANII "SUPERBA"
ASTRANTIA CARNIOLICA
HEMEROCALLIS "STELLA D'ORO"
PULMONARIA "ROY DAVIDSON"
LAVANDULA "HIDCOTE"
LAVANDULA "MUNSTEAD"
POTENTILLA FRUTICOSA
ROSMARINUS OFFICINALIS
ZANTEDESCHIA AETHIOPICA
BUDDLEIA DAVIDII
TAMARIX PENTANDRA
BUXUS SEMPERVIRENS
BUXUS MICROPHYLLA
HYDRANGEA PETIOLARIS
TRACHYCARPUS FORTUNEI
ROSA "GRAHAM THOMAS"
YUCCA GLAUCA
ARMERIA MARITIMA
CLEMATIS "NELLY MOSER"

SENECIO GREYI
FESTUCA GLAUCA
CLEMATIS MONTANA
LEWISIA COTYLEDON HYBRIDS
EUPHORBIA CHARACIAS WULFENII
TAXUS BACCATA "FASTIGIATA"

WISTERIA FLORIBUNDA
ABIES PINSAPO
ECHINOPS RITRO
ALLIUM GIGANTEUM
ARBUTUS UNEDO
SANTOLINA CHAMAECYPARISSUS

STYRAX JAPONICA
LAVANDULA STOECHAS
GAULTHERIA PROCUMBENS
CHAMAECYPARIS OBTUSA TETRAGONA AUREA
CEPHALOTAXUS HARRINGTONIA "FASTIGIATA"
LAVANDULA LAVATA

tentacles of *Helichrysum* 'Limelight', the burnished foliage and lavender flowers of *Heliotropium* 'Marine' and velvet spikes of *Salvia splendens* 'Royal Purple' almost obscure the front door. Bronze spears of *Phormium tenax* guard the small porch.

Branching off to one side, a narrow path squeezes between a tree peony crammed against the house and a vigorous climbing hydrangea scaling the fence on the other side. It leads to a walled garden made airy and spacious by changes of level and a palette of colour restricted to blues, pinks and purples with a touch of yellow here and there for contrast. Large fans of leaves visible from the street outside turn out to be a clump of four windmill palms crowded into a corner bed. Acquired when they were half their current size, they had to be lifted over the fence, and André cut the root balls in half to make them fit. None the worse for this

treatment, they tower 15 feet high over a skirt of bold-leafed *Hosta sieboldiana* which seems not to mind the dry soil.

More hostas, many with variegated cream and green leaves, run along the base of the wall under a *Hibiscus* 'Red Heart'. When the hibiscus blooms, its white and crimson flowers peep over the top of the hedge beside the palms. In fall, its leaves turn mustard yellow at the precise moment that the hostas below are following suit.

Underfoot the surface alternates between cement and rough squares of milky green slate, all painstakingly poured or cut and laid by André and Donna. They chose the slate with the idea that it could be easily taken up and repositioned as they developed a series of garden beds. but gradually the surface filled up with a range of containers which now hold most of the plants. Large terracotta urns bristle with small hebes like benign blue

hedgehogs or spill trickles of blue gentian and white lobelia; square planters hold clipped balls of boxwood; acid pink *Celosia* 'Flamingo Feather' and a burgundy-flowered nicotiana share a shallow bowl with blue spires of *Salvia farinacea* 'Victoria'. Donna likes to mix herbs in with the annuals, and admits to "getting all excited" if the combination of aromas and colours attracts the occasional monarch butterfly.

In a nook between garage and house, where a plate glass window once looked out on nothing but a blank wall, André has built a set of shelves to display his collection of bonsai. Miniature maples, a beech and a carefully shaped cotoneaster in glazed pots show off their intricate branch structure and gnarled roots during summer. In winter, they are moved to more protected quarters, and their place is taken by an assortment of hardy plants and a collection of small boulders, delicately coloured and veined. At the same time, lush leaves of golden hostas growing beneath the shelves die

back to reveal the spare beauty of smooth grey pebbles and craggy chunks of lava rock.

A white-painted pergola draped in wisteria creates a room for outdoor dining in the corner where two walls meet. Against one of the walls, a pair of topiary privet ascend in a series of clipped globes. Against the other, tall bronze fennel surrounds a giant terracotta pot, deliberately left empty to contrast with the overflow of smaller containers elsewhere in the garden. Where the pergola ends, 'John Davis' roses climb its supports, defining the enclosure and contributing a succession of tousled pink flowers and a spicy fragrance through summer and fall.

Glass doors overlooking the courtyard allow Donna and André to enjoy the view in all weathers. Only in fall, looking up beyond their walls to the vibrant red of the maple planted on the street outside, need they be reminded of how far they really are from more tropical zones. ❧

PAGE 110
A rosemary and pale green heads of *Sedum spectabile* share a corner with pots of clipped box.

PAGE 111
A head of Medusa presides over the courtyard.

PAGE 113
Trachycarpus palms and a yucca dominate the desert garden along the sidewalk.

PAGE 114
The rosy colour of shale brought from Saskatchewan highlights grey foliage of *Lavandula stoechas, Echinops ritro* and *Festuca glauca*.

PAGE 115
Topiaries of *Ligustrum japonicum* 'Texanum' frame a table under a pergola hung with wisteria.

ANDRE CHEVRIER AND DONNA DAVIS'S GARDEN

YAO-LIN CHU'S GARDEN: RIO VISTA

" . . . Precious qualities come by age, both of masonry and vegetation. The abrasion of hard edges and the falling out of mortar are a gain, for the lichen laps over the bruised moulding and the mortar is replaced by a cushion of moss." —GERTRUDE JEKYLL

A VANCOUVER LANDMARK, RIO VISTA shares with its sister mansion, Casa Mia, the distinction of being one of South Vancouver's most palatial properties. Built for sons of pioneer brewer Henry Reifel, the two properties were renowned for their conservatories and Pompeiian pools. During the 1940s they were highlights of the "Gardens Beautiful" tours conducted to aid the war effort, but in the years since that heyday, Rio Vista—the earlier and more impressive estate—has had its ups and downs

A grand vision in the Hollywood–Spanish Colonial style, the house boasts a long terrace of hexagonal tiles graced by statues of the four seasons on the north side, while, to the south, the precipitous terrain is cut into levels linked by flights of steps. Balustrades enclose each level, and line the sides of a viaduct which crosses the slope to the Pompeiian palm house and swimming pool with its adjoining garages.

Bought in 1972 by financier Joseph Segal, Rio Vista was subsequently landscaped by one of British Columbia's most famous garden designers, the late Raoul Robillard. It was Robillard who established the line of clipped holly behind wrought iron railings along the street frontage, and Robillard who introduced the massive rhododendrons — a west coast touch — that rise like an ocean swell against the holly. It was Segal who planned the curving tiers of steps descending to a wide level patio so that guests stepping out through the tall glass doors of the ground floor ballroom could have an area to stroll in the cool night air.

The focus of the house is toward this side garden

AIRPORT

NATIVE GARDEN
PSEUDOTSUGA MENZIESII 90' HT.
THUJA PLICATA
TSUGA HETEROPHYLLA
ACER MACROPHYLLUM
MAHONIA AQUIFOLIUM
SAMBUCUS RACEMOSA
POLYSTICHUM MUNITUM
BLECHNUM SPICANT
GAULTHERIA SHALLON
CORYLUS CORNUTA
TOLMIEA MENZIESII
CORNUS NUTTALLII
ACER PALMATUM

PLANTS IN GARDEN
ENKIANTHUS CAMPANULATUS
PHOTINIA X FRASERI
BUXUS SEMPERVIRENS
COTONEASTER HORIZONTALIS
CHAMAECYPARIS PISIFERA 'FILIFERA AUREA'
CEDRUS ATLANTICA 'GLAUCA' 80' HT.
CHAMAECYPARIS OBTUSA 'NANA'
ACER PALMATUM 'ATROPURPUREUM'
SEQUOIADENDRON GIGANTEUM 'PENDULUM'
CEDRUS DEODARA
CEDRUS LIBANI
ILEX CRENATA 'CONVEXA'
CAMELLIA JAPONICA (CULTIVARS)

ACER PALMATUM 'DISSECTUM ATROPURPUREUM'
CHAMAECYPARIS PISIFERA 'BOULEVARD'
MAGNOLIA SOULANGIANA
CORNUS FLORIDA
CHAMAECYPARIS PISIFERA 'PLUMOSA'
HOSTA SIEBOLDIANA 'ELEGANS'
THUJA OCCIDENTALIS 'WOODWARDII'
TAXUS BACCATA 'ADPRESSA'
CHAMAECYPARIS OBTUSA 'CORALLIFORMIS'
AUCUBA JAPONICA 'PICTURATA'
PRUNUS CERASIFERA 'PISSARDII'
CHAMAECYPARIS PISIFERA 'FILIFERA'
X OSMAREA BURKWOODII

NATIVE GARDEN

SUNKEN GARDEN

GREENHOUSE

CONSERVATORY
TOP LEVEL

COACH HOUSE

PORTE
COCHERE

SWIMMING POOL
BOTTOM LEVEL

BRIDGE

RESIDENCE

Rio Vista

LOWER PATIO
OFF BALLROOM

TENNIS COURT

FRONT ENTRANCE

UPPER PATIO

←— 285 —→

5 PRUNUS CERASIFERA PISSARDII

S.

E.   W.

N.

PLANTS IN FRONT GARDEN
FOTHERGILLA MAJOR
HEDGES - EAST & WEST - THUJA PLICATA
HEDRA HELIX (GROUND COVER)
PRUNUS LUSITANICA (DRIVEWAY HEDGE)
ILEX AQUIFOLIUM (HEDGE BEHIND FENCE)
WISTERIA FLORIBUNDA
FORSYTHIA X INTERMEDIA
VIBURNUM DAVIDII

NANDINA DOMESTICA
HYDRANGEA MACROPHYLLA
FATSIA JAPONICA
PRUNUS CERASIFERA
PHILADELPHUS CORONARIUS
SYRINGA VULGARIS (OLD CULTIVARS)
PICEA PUNGENS 'GLAUCA'
PINUS SYLVESTRIS

PIERIS JAPONICA
AZALEA MOLLIS
CRYPTOMERIA JAPONICA 'BANDAI SUGI'
RHODODENDRON 'ELIZABETH'
RHODODENDRON AUGUSTINII
RHODODENDRON PONTICUM
PRUNUS LAUROCERASUS
ILEX AQUIFOLIUM 'ARGENTEA MARGINATA'

"The palms in the palm house all come from the set of a movie shot here. It's bad Feng Shui to have a plant die in your house, so I rescued them, and now they are all doing well."

where the fall of land makes a dramatic curve down from the end of the north terrace. A row of weeping sequoiadendrons dances down the far side of the steps like a corps-de-ballet. From the patio, guests can gaze up at these contorted shapes against the sky or, turning the other way, look out over a series of cascades falling over rocks and through pools until the inky water swirls away under the arcades of the viaduct. Trails of ivy festoon wrought-iron chandeliers hanging in the centre of each of the three arches. The scene is so reminiscent of old paintings of arcadian landscapes, you almost expect to see a shepherd lad and lass leaning against a distant tree trunk.

Yao-Lin Chu, whose family bought Rio Vista in 1989, shakes his head at the invasion of the ivy. Although two full-time workers care for the grounds, nature is quick to reclaim any area momentarily forgotten. It's the same in the small circular garden enclosed by a dry stone wall which separates it from the nearby waterfall: as fast as ivy is cleared from the vertical faces, the vining stems launch another attack. A stone gryphon stands here in a circle of buttercups. Above the wall, brown trunks of rhododendrons make arabesques against their canopy of dark foliage.

Yao-Lin and his sister are gradually restoring the garden, beginning four years ago with an overhaul of the beautiful palm house. Hand-painted tiles surrounding its rectangular pool have been repaired and cleaned, and a wealth of tropical plants basks on its balconies. Many of these were left behind in the aftermath of a movie filmed on site. Neglected to the point of death, they have been coaxed back to flourishing health under Yao-Lin's supervision.

Beyond the palm house, small paths descend the

slope among a forest of fir and maple that has grown up on the steep embankment, obscuring much of the view across the Fraser River and the distant Gulf of Georgia. The best views are still to be had from the formal terraced garden that occupies level ground one flight below the long arcade of a porte-cochere that protects the main south entrance to the house. Ornate wrought iron arches mark the top of steps leading to this small grassy terrace enclosed by a heavy concrete balustrade that matches the one on the level above. In the centre of an apron of grass, canna lilies occupy a rectangular bed. A curved stone seat at one end is sup-

ported by gryphons, a recurring motif at Rio Vista. At the other end, a blue Atlas cedar rises from one level to another, reaching up past the top of the viaduct to the balcony above the porte-cochere. Its massive size suggests that it was planted when the house was new, perhaps to aid the illusion of a Tuscan hillside.

Few gardens in Vancouver reflect the influence of the Renaissance gardens of northern Italy as clearly as those of Rio Vista. Those who think its style is out of place in the west coast landscape might be surprised at how well it marries with the flat fields below, outlined here and there by long rows of Lombardy poplars. ᴄ⅌

JOSEPH SEGAL'S GARDEN

*"If you're going to do it 90% of the way,
you might as well do it 100% of the way—
or leave it the way it was."*

SCALLOPED DOWN THE STEEP HILL-side above Spanish Banks, the lush flowerbeds and mature trees of the Segal estate belie the short span of time—a mere four years—that they have been in place. While the palatial house, a modern interpretation of a Roman villa, was being completed, Joe Segal was busy rescuing trees and shrubs from demolition sites throughout the city, holding them in readiness for the day that landscaping could begin.

Thus the waterfall that spills over a huge slab of Squamish rock in the curve of circular driveway is surrounded by rare conifers like *Chamaecyparis nootkatensis* 'Pendula' and a total of four *Sequoiadendron giganteum* 'Pendulum'. Through their cool shade, a shaft of sunlight strikes the glassy surface of the

pond into which the filtered, tempera-ture-controlled water trickles. The Segals used to stock the pond with koi, but, despite a system of motion-sensitive water jets that slash the air just above the surface, successive raid-ing parties of raccoons and herons thwarted this scheme; now only slivers of neon-bright goldfish flash in the depths.

Across the paved driveway, a path steps down between tall stands of golden bamboo that provide a living curtain each side of the massive front door, and the same colour frosts the tips of several *Cryptomeria japonica* 'Aurea' that frame the windows on either side.

Behind one of the bamboo screens, a small courtyard, accessible only from inside the house, protects a citrus orchard in terracotta pots. Limes, lemons, oranges,

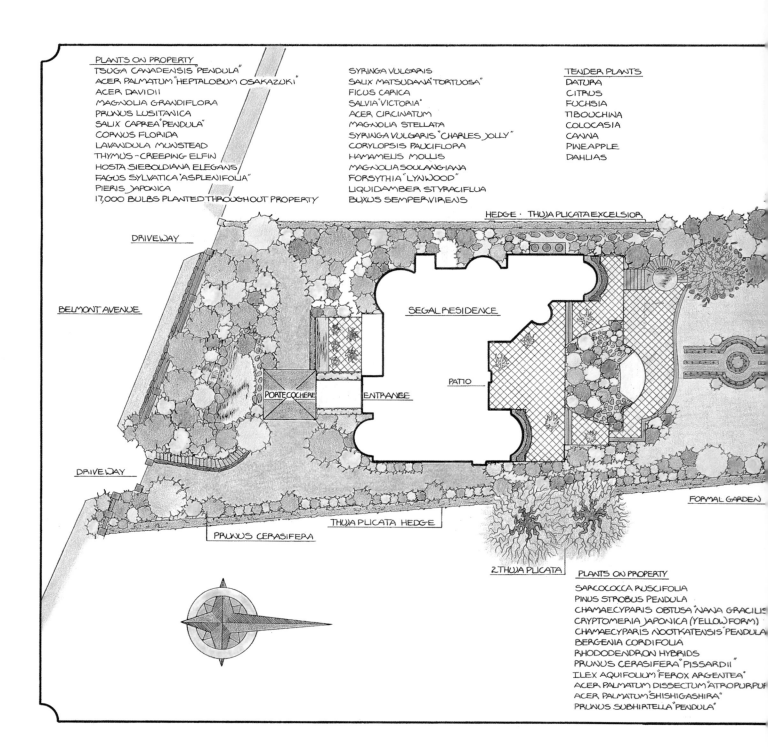

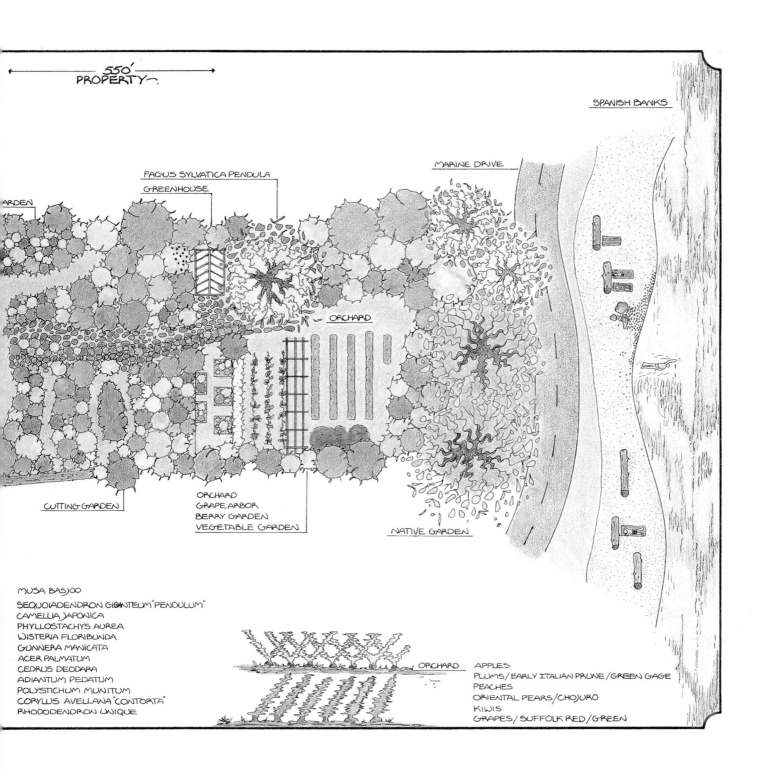

550'
PROPERTY

SPANISH BANKS

MARINE DRIVE

FAGUS SYLVATICA PENDULA
GREENHOUSE

ARDEN

ORCHARD

CUTTING GARDEN

ORCHARD
GRAPE ARBOR
BERRY GARDEN
VEGETABLE GARDEN

NATIVE GARDEN

MUSA BASJOO
SEQUOIADENDRON GIGANTEUM "PENDULUM"
CAMELLIA JAPONICA
PHYLLOSTACHYS AUREA
WISTERIA FLORIBUNDA
GUNNERA MANICATA
ACER PALMATUM
CEDRUS DEODARA
ADIANTUM PEDATUM
POLYSTICHUM MUNITUM
CORYLUS AVELLANA "CONTORTA"
RHODODENDRON UNIQUE

ORCHARD

ORCHARD
APPLES
PLUMS/EARLY ITALIAN PRUNE/GREEN GAGE
PEACHES
ORIENTAL PEARS/CHOJURO
KIWIS
GRAPES/SUFFOLK RED/GREEN

grapefruit—even a pineapple—thrive and produce fruit in this little sun trap. The retaining wall that hides this retreat from the drive is overhung with wisteria dangling down towards its own reflection in a long, narrow rectangle of water. Two terracotta plinths hold planters awash with pelargoniums, lobelia and Swan River daisies to add some colour to the composition when the wisteria flowers have come and gone.

A canopy of magnolias and bronze-leaved maples shades the narrow path that leads from the courtyard around the side of the house, past a huge banana plant with leaves like half-furled green sails. The sense of enclosure is enhanced by a terraced bank enveloped in ivy and trailing fuchsias. However, as the path descends, following the line of the fence, it changes character: rough flagstones are outlined in clumps of variegated grass and a rustic wooden hand rail offers support where slope changes to steps. Of this area Joe Segal says, "I want it to look natural, not manicured. It can be a hodgepodge, but it must be a natural hodgepodge."

The manicure is reserved for the broad swath of green lawn that opens out from the foot of the side path and spreads across the full width of the property. Rising at random from it, the shaggy shapes of more sequoias frame a panoramic view across English Bay to the mountains. At the centre of the lawn, a classic parterre glows like a jewelled medallion. Its shape is defined by clipped box but, like much of the planting in this area, the colours are determined by a succession of bulbs and annuals that change with the seasons. When I visited in midsummer, pale pink begonias and tufts of blue fescue made the pattern, punctuated by the grey trunks and hanging pink trumpets of *Brugmansia*.

A semi-circular patio opening from the main floor of the house provides a vantage point for admiring the pattern of the parterre, or for gazing out at the North Shore mountains that make a wide-screen backdrop to the house and garden. The patio itself is large enough to

peeled branches is slotted through rough cedar uprights. A thin ribbon of heather runs like a green shadow beneath the railing.

On either side of the descending slope, massive cubes of bevelled concrete form retaining walls for small pockets of level ground holding plants for cutting or plots of fruit and vegetables. A bed of long-stemmed hybrid tea roses here, waving blades of gladiolus foliage there; a row of raspberries, raised beds of carrots and beets, and a long strip of strawberries on one side, a greenhouse full of melon vines, cucumbers and tomatoes on the other. A massive 'Concord' grape spans the gap from one level to another, parsley planted at the foot of its shaggy trunk. On a lower plateau, more grapes and kiwis occupy a pergola, and at the very bottom of the long descent, dwarf fruit trees line up in neat rows on a stretch of sunlit grass. Most are apples, but there is room for peaches, pears and cherries too.

Beyond this orchard, a row of large pines defines the northern edge of the property, underplanted with a variety of rhododendrons that weren't sufficiently attractive to merit a more prominent position on the estate.

On the way back up, Joe Segal points out a wide-spreading walnut tree from which he says he has never harvested a nut, although he feeds "the entire squirrel population with that one tree." Not far away on the western boundary, a weeping beech hangs over banks of deep red rhododendrons. It is the only tree that was on the property when the Segals bought it. Joe Segal remembers the way the land looked then. "It was just one big hill," he says. "Now, it's like a different world." ♋

include its own garden beds, a riot of colourful annuals and tender perennials that also change with the seasons. "Why have a patio without any life or colour on it?" is Joe Segal's rhetorical question as he surveys the summer planting: blue salvias, pink dahlias, scarlet impatiens and the dusky purple fans of canna leaves creating a fiery contrast to the monochrome of lawn below, while echoing the brilliant colours of the parterre that bisects it. Even close to the house, where garden beds yield to cool, cream-coloured tiles defining the entertaining area, an assortment of fuchsias and pelargoniums spills from huge planters of terracotta or English lead, and under the tall cylindrical windows of the house a curve of bright tuberous begonias sparkles against a ribbon of sweet box (*Sarcococca ruscifolia*).

Two curving staircases link the patio with the lawn, which is wrapped on the other side by a border of perennials broken by what appears to be the beginning of a path. Here, an undulating carpet of thyme, punctuated by rough-cut grey basalt stones, begins to unroll down the steep slope until stopped by a row of rhododendrons and pines far below. Down the centre, a rustic railing of

RUDI PINKOWSKI'S GARDEN

"A garden should be an escape from everyday life."

WHEN RUDI PINKOWSKI ARRIVES home, he wants to feel that he is entering a tropical resort. To achieve this illusion he has created a garden of large, lush-leaved plants high on the North Shore mountains overlooking Burrard Inlet. The distant views of water with the city laid out beyond are filtered through a screen of eucalyptus leaves and framed by the solid trunks of banana palms. Not all the plants are imports from warmer climes, however—as Rudi points out, natives of the northern rainforests also blend well into a jungle theme. There is space here for skunk cabbage with its substantial spatulas of bright green leaf, and the spiny stems and jagged leaves of devil's club, although Rudi grows the latter in a pot to control its invasive tendencies. Even rhododendrons, maples and native ferns settle comfortably among the more exotic yuccas and canna lilies.

There were more rhododendrons in Rudi's original design. "When I came here, I was crazy about them," Rudi reveals, "but after 20 years I got rhododendron fatigue." It is 10 years since he began to completely remake the garden into the lush and vivid landscape it is today.

Rudi's strong belief in the importance of contributing to the neighbourhood dictates that his garden should begin at the very edge of the sidewalk. Here a massing of plants sweeps up and back to partially screen the house from view. Low-growing ferns sprout around yuccas, azaleas, a Hinoki cypress and a young monkey puzzle tree. A tree fern (*Dicksonia antarctica*) sparkles in the sunshine against a backdrop of large rhododendrons, which Rudi has chosen specifically for early bloom on the principle that "people like to get a wake-up in spring."

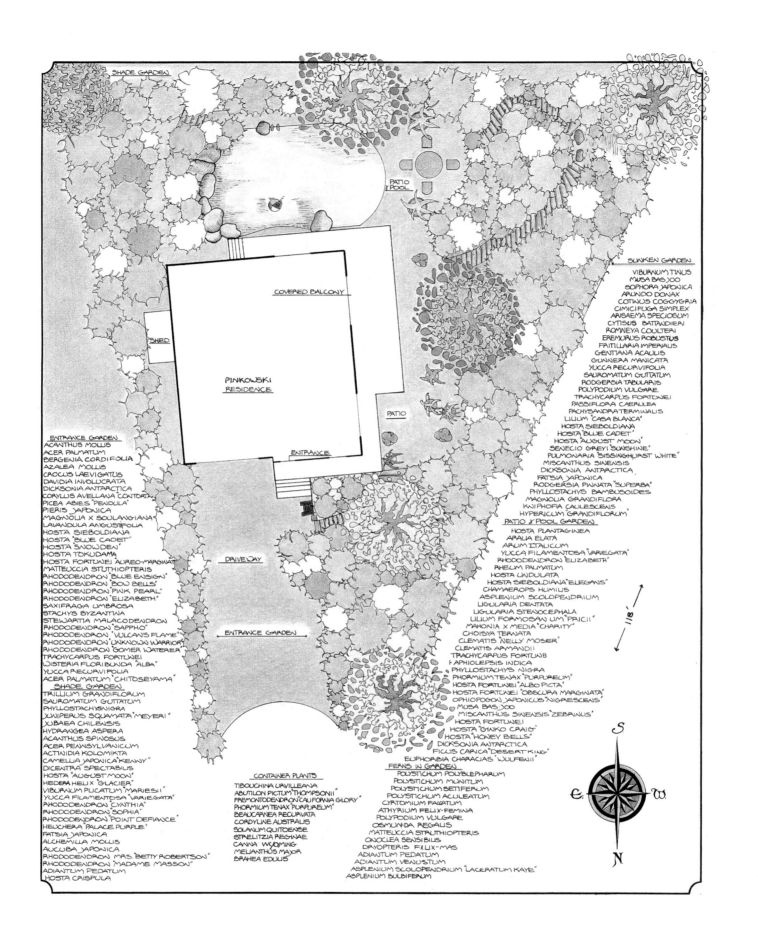

SHADE GARDEN

PATIO
& POOL

COVERED BALCONY

SHED

PINKOWSKI
RESIDENCE

PATIO

ENTRANCE

ENTRANCE GARDEN
ACANTHUS MOLLIS
ACER PALMATUM
BERGENIA CORDIFOLIA
AZALEA MOLLIS
CROCUS LAEVIGATUS
DAVIDIA INVOLUCRATA
DICKSONIA ANTARCTICA
CORYLUS AVELLANA CONTORTA
PICEA ABIES 'PENDULA'
PIERIS JAPONICA
MAGNOLIA X SOULANGIANA
LAVANDULA ANGUSTIFOLIA
HOSTA SIEBOLDIANA
HOSTA 'BLUE CADET'
HOSTA 'SNOWDEN'
HOSTA TOKUDAMA
HOSTA FORTUNEI AUREO-MARGINATA
MATTEUCCIA STRUTHIOPTERIS
RHODODENDRON 'BLUE ENSIGN'
RHODODENDRON 'BOW BELLS'
RHODODENDRON 'PINK PEARL'
RHODODENDRON 'ELIZABETH'
SAXIFRAGA UMBROSA
STACHYS BYZANTINA
STEWARTIA MALACODENDRON
RHODODENDRON 'SAPPHO'
RHODODENDRON 'VULCAN'S FLAME'
RHODODENDRON 'UNKNOWN WARRIOR'
RHODODENDRON 'GOMER WATERER'
TRACHYCARPUS FORTUNEI
WISTERIA FLORIBUNDA 'ALBA'
YUCCA RECURVIFOLIA
ACER PALMATUM 'CHITOSEYAMA'
SHADE GARDEN
TRILLIUM GRANDIFLORUM
SAUROMATUM GUTTATUM
PHYLLOSTACHYS NIGRA
JUNIPERUS SQUAMATA 'MEYERI'
JUBAEA CHILENSIS
HYDRANGEA ASPERA
ACANTHUS SPINOSUS
ACER PENNSYLVANICUM
ACTINIDIA KOLOMIKTA
CAMELLIA JAPONICA 'KENNY'
DICENTRA SPECTABILIS
HOSTA 'AUGUST MOON'
HEDERA HELIX X 'GLACIER'
VIBURNUM PLICATUM 'MARIESII'
YUCCA FILAMENTOSA 'VARIEGATA'
RHODODENDRON 'CYNTHIA'
RHODODENDRON 'SOPHIA'
RHODODENDRON 'POINT DEFIANCE'
HEUCHERA 'PALACE PURPLE'
FATSIA JAPONICA
ALCHEMILLA MOLLIS
AUCUBA JAPONICA
RHODODENDRON 'MRS. BETTY ROBERTSON'
RHODODENDRON 'MADAME MASSON'
ADIANTUM PEDATUM
HOSTA CRISPULA

DRIVEWAY

ENTRANCE GARDEN

CONTAINER PLANTS
TIBOUCHINA URVILLEANA
ABUTILON PICTUM 'THOMPSONII'
FREMONTODENDRON 'CALIFORNIA GLORY'
PHORMIUM TENAX 'PURPUREUM'
BEAUCARNEA RECURVATA
CORDYLINE AUSTRALIS
SOLANUM QUITOENSE
STRELITZIA REGINAE
CANNA 'WYOMING'
MELIANTHUS MAJOR
BRAHEA EDULIS

SUNKEN GARDEN
VIBURNUM TINUS
MUSA BASJOO
SOPHORA JAPONICA
ARUNDO DONAX
COTINUS COGGYGRIA
CIMICIFUGA SIMPLEX
ARISAEMA SPECIOSUM
CYTISUS BATTANDIERI
ROMNEYA COULTERI
EREMURUS ROBUSTUS
FRITILLARIA IMPERIALIS
GENTIANA ACAULIS
GUNNERA MANICATA
YUCCA RECURVIFOLIA
SAUROMATUM GUTTATUM
RODGERSIA TABULARIS
POLYPODIUM VULGARE
TRACHYCARPUS FORTUNEI
PASSIFLORA CAERULEA
PACHYSANDRA TERMINALIS
LILIUM 'CASA BLANCA'
HOSTA SIEBOLDIANA
HOSTA 'BLUE CADET'
HOSTA 'AUGUST MOON'
SENECIO GREYI 'SUNSHINE'
PULMONARIA 'SISSINGHURST WHITE'
MISCANTHUS SINENSIS
DICKSONIA ANTARCTICA
FATSIA JAPONICA
RODGERSIA PINNATA 'SUPERBA'
PHYLLOSTACHYS BAMBUSOIDES
MAGNOLIA GRANDIFLORA
KNIPHOFIA CAULESCENS
HYPERICUM GRANDIFLORUM
PATIO & POOL GARDEN
HOSTA PLANTAGINEA
ARALIA ELATA
ARUM ITALICUM
YUCCA FILAMENTOSA 'VARIEGATA'
RHODODENDRON 'ELIZABETH'
RHEUM PALMATUM
HOSTA UNDULATA
HOSTA SIEBOLDIANA 'ELEGANS'
CHAMAEROPS HUMILIS
ASPLENIUM SCOLOPENDRIUM
LIGULARIA DENTATA
LIGULARIA STENOCEPHALA
LILIUM FORMOSANUM 'PRICII'
MAHONIA X MEDIA 'CHARITY'
CHOISYA TERNATA
CLEMATIS 'NELLY MOSER'
CLEMATIS ARMANDII
TRACHYCARPUS FORTUNEI
RAPHIOLEPSIS INDICA
PHYLLOSTACHYS NIGRA
PHORMIUM TENAX 'PURPUREUM'
HOSTA FORTUNEI 'ALBO PICTA'
HOSTA FORTUNEI 'OBSCURA MARGINATA'
OPHIOPOGON JAPONICUS 'NIGRESCENS'
MUSA BASJOO
MISCANTHUS SINENSIS 'ZEBRINUS'
HOSTA FORTUNEI
HOSTA 'GINKO CRAIG'
HOSTA 'HONEY BELLS'
DICKSONIA ANTARCTICA
FICUS CARICA 'DESERT KING'
EUPHORBIA CHARACIAS 'WULFENII'
FERNS IN GARDEN
POLYSTICHUM POLYBLEPHARUM
POLYSTICHUM MUNITUM
POLYSTICHUM SETIFERUM
POLYSTICHUM ACULEATUM
CYRTOMIUM FALCATUM
ATHYRIUM FELIX-FEMINA
POLYPODIUM VULGARE
OSMUNDA REGALIS
MATTEUCCIA STRUTHIOPTERIS
ONOCLEA SENSIBILIS
DRYOPTERIS FILIX-MAS
ADIANTUM PEDATUM
ADIANTUM VENUSTUM
ASPLENIUM SCOLOPENDRIUM 'LACERATUM KAYE'
ASPLENIUM BULBIFERUM

118'

S
E — W
N

An empress tree (*Pawlonia tomentosa*) presides over the bed, its wide-spreading crown decked in spring with candles of lavender-blue flowers. Beside its mottled trunk, steep steps descend alongside the dappled shade of a bank where a few of the tree's large roots lie like alligators among clumps of sword fern and variegated hostas. On top of the bank, the rhododendrons that frame the street planting have been trimmed of their lower branches to reveal a fretwork of cinnamon-brown undulating trunks. As they grow taller, Rudi will fill in underneath them with more ferns. It is a technique that he has used extensively throughout the garden to enhance the jungle effect.

Where the steps end on a wide patio, an aralia, easily 20 feet tall, caps its own pair of high-rising, grey stems with a lacy umbrella of foliage and pinwheels of creamy flower. Baskets and tubs of bright-flowered annuals mark the end of the descent and the change from shady grove to open ground. Impatiens, pelargoniums and petunias dazzle the eyes with hues of hot pink, purple and golden yellow. Among the black silk arrowheads of a taro lily and the tiger-striped leaves of tall cannas lurks one of the three household cats—somehow more tigerlike itself in this environment.

There is a fig tree here, and a kiwi vine "because it's nice to have some edibles," and masses of Oriental lilies, chosen for their satin colours and heady fragrance on summer evenings.

Rudi has designed this part of the garden, which surrounds the turquoise rectangle of a swimming pool, so that, even in the midst of Vancouver's rainy season, he can enjoy the lushness of vegetation from a dry haven inside the house. For this reason, too, over half the plants in view are evergreen, and they are planted thickly for a luxuriant, though not overgrown, effect. Rough chunks of pink granite edge the beds and pile up above one end of the pool where a waterfall and a river of ivy gush over them. A *Tibouchina urvilleana* graces the crest of the granite wall with flowers of vivid purple studding its sombre foliage. On the long side of the pool, a stand of banana palms demands attention for the

the *Tibouchina,* imposing rhododendrons, once again pruned to reveal their trunks at eye-level, crowd the edges of a path that winds under lofty Douglas firs. It's dark in here, brightened only by a drift of lime-green hostas glowing among the underplanting of ferns. But where the narrow path comes to an end at the wall of the house, you come face to face with the startling contrast of a sunshine-yellow chair. It is there, Rudi explains, to act as the flash of a bird's yellow bill would act on an explorer of the Amazon's gloomy depths.

At the other end of the pool, framing the far-away blue sea, stand two tall palms (*Cordyline australis*), fountains of bronze on slender, ribbed trunks. They help to define the edge of the patio where the ground drops steeply away down a near-vertical cliff, criss-crossed by a winding track. A waterfall tumbles down the face of the cliff towards a deep, still pool at its base. The southwest aspect makes the soil very dry near the top of the descent, and allows Rudi the opportunity to plant prickly pear, New Zealand silverbush, yuccas and a pineapple broom. As you follow the path downward, however, these desert lovers give way to ferns, hostas and voodoo lilies, and the illusion of tropical rainforest once again takes hold. At the edge of the pool the huge, ragged leaves of *Gunnera manicata* loom overhead on thick, spiny stalks that are reflected faintly in the limpid dark water.

A different route leads upwards into the light once again, emerging farther along the patio with its bird's eye view of Burrard Inlet. Surrounded by luxuriant growth and the vivid colours of tropical blooms, even a bird must find it difficult to remember that on the other side of the house, the snowline of Grouse Mountain begins at the top of the street. ❧

sheer size of their leaves, half-furled scrolls of snakeskin green. "The queen of foliage," Rudi calls them. He has placed them by the pool to encourage visitors' desire to swim—"If they were pine trees, you wouldn't get that same feeling."

Close to the house under a balcony, a collection of pots holds tender plants that also conjure up visions of South Seas islands: young palms, a bird-of-paradise plant (*Strelitzia reginae*), more cannas and a *Fremontodendron* with flowers the colour of lemonade.

Beyond one end of the pool, on the heights behind

GERARD PURY'S GARDEN

"I'm like a stamp collector. If there's a plant I like then I have to get it, even if I don't know where to put it."

Along the ribs of the spine of Main Street where east Vancouver meets west, many of the houses are still small post-war bungalows, sitting neatly on squares of lawn among a rhododendron or two, with a line of annuals flanking the path that runs straight from sidewalk to front door. This makes Gerard Pury's place clearly visible from the end of the block. He has no lawn; he has a jungle, bursting luxuriantly into the air and out to the edge of the curb.

Huge *Trachycarpus* palms—some twice the height of the roofline—engulf the house, their trunks awash in billows of knee-high impatiens in tropical colours of red, orange and purple. The arm of a weeping Cedar of Lebanon reaches out from behind a wall of foliage and swathes the Kwanzan cherry on the boulevard in a veil of blue. An enormous moss basket, also loaded with impatiens, is lashed to a branch of the cherry by heavy chains.

Peach-coloured trumpets of brugmansia hang over the edge of the sidewalk, dousing it in their fragrance at night. Lower down, big lilypad leaves of *Petasites japonicus* var. *giganteus* jostle against a confining hedge of variegated holly (*Ilex 'Ferox Argentea'*), its clipped geometry a counterpoint to the lush exuberance of ferns and palms. Gerard has tried to remove the *Petasites*—"it's not quite a noxious weed"—but every speck left in the ground generates new growth in spring. Nevertheless, he thinks it is underused as a container plant, and has one growing in a large pot by the front door. There its structural qualities can shine but it cannot indulge its invasive habits.

Also confined, in a large stone trough, is a Ponderosa pine that has been growing there for more than 20

137

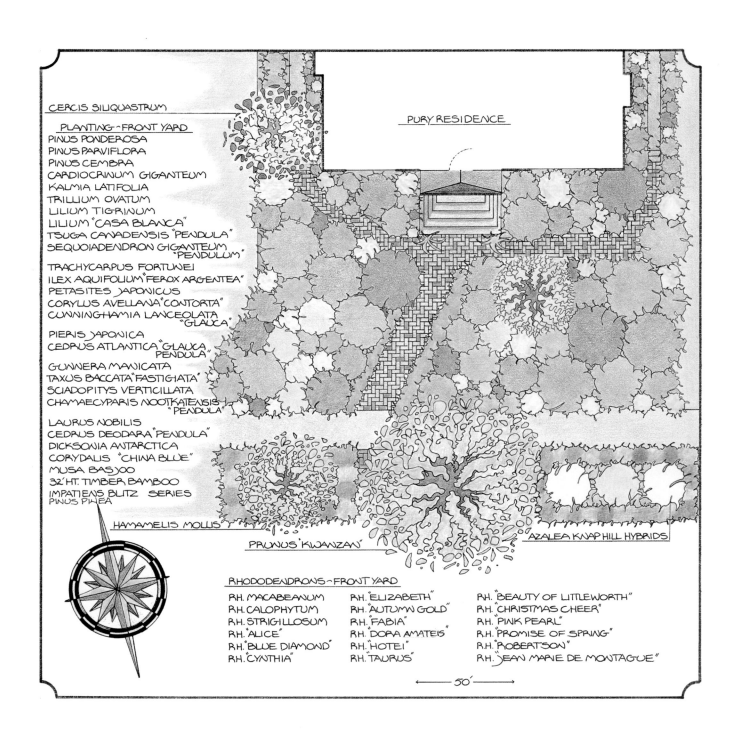

CERCIS SILIQUASTRUM

PURY RESIDENCE

PLANTING ~ FRONT YARD
PINUS PONDEROSA
PINUS PARVIFLORA
PINUS CEMBRA
CARDIOCRINUM GIGANTEUM
KALMIA LATIFOLIA
TRILLIUM OVATUM
LILIUM TIGRINUM
LILIUM "CASA BLANCA"
TSUGA CANADENSIS "PENDULA"
SEQUOIADENDRON GIGANTEUM
                    "PENDULUM"

TRACHYCARPUS FORTUNEI
ILEX AQUIFOLIUM "FEROX ARGENTEA"
PETASITES JAPONICUS
CORYLUS AVELLANA "CONTORTA"
CUNNINGHAMIA LANCEOLATA
                    "GLAUCA"

PIERIS JAPONICA
CEDRUS ATLANTICA "GLAUCA
                    PENDULA"
GUNNERA MANICATA
TAXUS BACCATA "FASTIGIATA"
SCIADOPITYS VERTICILLATA
CHAMAECYPARIS NOOTKATENSIS
                    "PENDULA"

LAURUS NOBILIS
CEDRUS DEODARA "PENDULA"
DICKSONIA ANTARCTICA
CORYDALIS "CHINA BLUE"
MUSA BASJOO
32' HT. TIMBER BAMBOO
IMPATIENS BLITZ SERIES
PINUS PINEA

HAMAMELIS MOLLIS

PRUNUS "KWANZAN"

AZALEA KNAP HILL HYBRIDS

RHODODENDRONS ~ FRONT YARD

RH. MACABEANUM	RH. "ELIZABETH"	RH. "BEAUTY OF LITTLEWORTH"
RH. CALOPHYTUM	RH. "AUTUMN GOLD"	RH. "CHRISTMAS CHEER"
RH. STRIGILLOSUM	RH. "FABIA"	RH. "PINK PEARL"
RH. "ALICE"	RH. "DORA AMATEIS"	RH. "PROMISE OF SPRING"
RH. "BLUE DIAMOND"	RH. "HOTEI"	RH. "ROBERTSON"
RH. "CYNTHIA"	RH. "TAURUS"	RH. "JEAN MARIE DE MONTAGUE"

←——— 50' ———→

years. The process has served to keep its growth short and send its branches out at twisted angles, like an oversized bonsai specimen.

There are still a few rhododendrons, remnants of Gerard's first passion, jammed among the palms and groves of bananas, but now they must hold their own with Tasmanian tree ferns (*Dicksonia antarctica*), an assortment of pines including a Mediterranean stone pine (*Pinus pinea*), a *Cunninghamia lanceolata*, a weeping hemlock, a contorted hazel and a stand of bamboo as high as the flagpole that stands beside it. In and around their trunks, tiger lilies seed themselves with abandon and the exotic bells of pink abutilon sprout from willowy stems. Everywhere between are the impatiens, a German-bred variety known as 'Blitz', — so dense a swirl of vivid colour that it brightens the darkest nooks.

Along the property line on either side, plants spill over neighbouring lawns. A large *Brugmansia versicolor* with flowers like golden champagne flutes has to be restrained by a leash anchoring it to a nearby pine. A Judas tree (*Cercis siliquastrum*) spreads widely above. Gerard has pruned it once since he planted it in 1965, but he did so reluctantly because he likes its natural shape. On the other side of the garden a low retaining wall curbs the bamboo and checks the enthusiasm of *Acanthus mollis* and castor bean (*Rheum palmatum*). "This wasn't planned," says Gerard. "My original idea was to replace the lawn with a fish pond and a waterfall, but suddenly I needed the room for the plants."

At the side of the house, the teeming growth of the front garden gives way to what Gerard likes to call his "playground." A narrow path squeezes between a thriving bay laurel and volunteer hellebores against the wall of the house. On its other side row upon row of black pots filled with seedling tree ferns, monkey puzzle trees and palms are ranked against the property line. A tall bamboo grass (*Arundo donax*) rustles overhead, its questing roots safely contained within a five-gallon pot.

Many more large specimens fill the small back yard, grudging some space to the much-abbreviated vegetable garden and a tiny patch of grass. "It was all vegetable garden once," the owner says ruefully. "Somehow I started growing these plants, but I miss my vegetables." There is still room for a European quince, however, and every fall Gerard's wife spends hours turning its prolific output into jelly. Space is also accorded to a compost pile, a modest greenhouse and a Swiss chalet of a garden shed, a gesture to Gerard's birthplace. The original *Trachycarpus* seed came from Switzerland, too, in 1966, pocketed by Gerard as he passed a hotel display. Now he has so many, he hardly knows what to do with them. It takes him five years to raise each plant to a size strong enough to survive a Vancouver winter without protection. In the meantime, he stacks the young ones underneath his back porch in winter, where they manage quite nicely with an occasional watering.

Other exotic treasures include black taro plants (*Colocasia esculenta*), cannas with burnished burgundy leaves, and New Zealand flax (*Phormium tenax*) with spikes of pink and copper like a south seas sunset. The graceful silhouette of a silk tree (*Albizia julibrissin*) holds a filigree of finely cut leaves above clumps of hibiscus and hart's tongue fern, while at the very back of the property a young *Paulownia tomentosa* sends a majestic spike skyward, looking very much like the early stages of Jack's beanstalk. It marks the spot where its parent once overflowed its container, sending roots down into the soft surrounding earth. Although the original is long gone, young plants continue to emerge in the area with admirable persistence.

Leaving Gerard Pury's garden, through the brilliance of the front garden, conjures up a memory of the words on Christopher Wren's tomb in St. Paul's Cathedral: "If my memorial you seek, look around you." Up and down the block, almost every garden, however minimal, is sporting one or two young *Trachycarpus* palms. ❧

PAGE 136
A banana plant and tiger lilies loom over a carpet of impatiens.

PAGE 137
Petasites japonicus imprisoned in a sturdy pot on the front steps.

PAGE 139 ABOVE
The pendant trumpets of *Brugmansia versicolor.*

PAGE 139 BELOW
A rare *Tsuga canadensis* 'Pendula' behind *Brugmansia versicolor* and the broad leaves of a *Gunnera manicata.*

PAGE 141
Even the boulevard cherry tree is hung with baskets of impatiens.

THOMAS HOBBS'S GARDEN

*"I wanted a Mediterranean look to go with the house.
That means choosing plants with tropical-looking foliage that will
grow in this climate. It's all about faking it."*

THE HOUSE, DUBBED KANIA Castle for the man who built it, is one of Vancouver's best examples of the Spanish Colonial style of architecture which reached its zenith in the California of the roaring twenties. From where it sits, on a triangle of land high above the beaches of West Point Grey, the panorama over English Bay toward the towers of downtown, the North Shore mountains and out to sea is breathtaking.

Designing a garden equal to the eccentricity of the house and the grandeur of the view is a formidable undertaking, but one that Thomas Hobbs has approached with his usual gusto. Well-known in Vancouver for dramatic designs during his career as a florist, the man who "always wanted to own a nursery," and now does, has turned his own garden into a showcase for the unusual, the bold and the beautiful.

On its flat-iron corner with the land dropping steeply to the north, the house basks among tall windmill palms, the iron railings of its balconies above the front door draped in the sinuous stems of a white *Akebia quinata* vine and the gnarled canes of a climbing rose whose flowers are also white. "Just as well," says the owner. "If they had turned out to be red, it would have had to go." Thomas Hobbs has strong likes and dislikes, and red is not a favourite colour, but it is the clash with the terracotta-washed walls of the house that would have doomed the rose.

There is no sidewalk around the house, but a pattern of large sandstone squares, wide at the curb, narrowing abruptly towards the black iron gate, is set into a carpet of thyme to provide dry footing as well as a sense of ceremony to the approach. On either side, the slate-blue

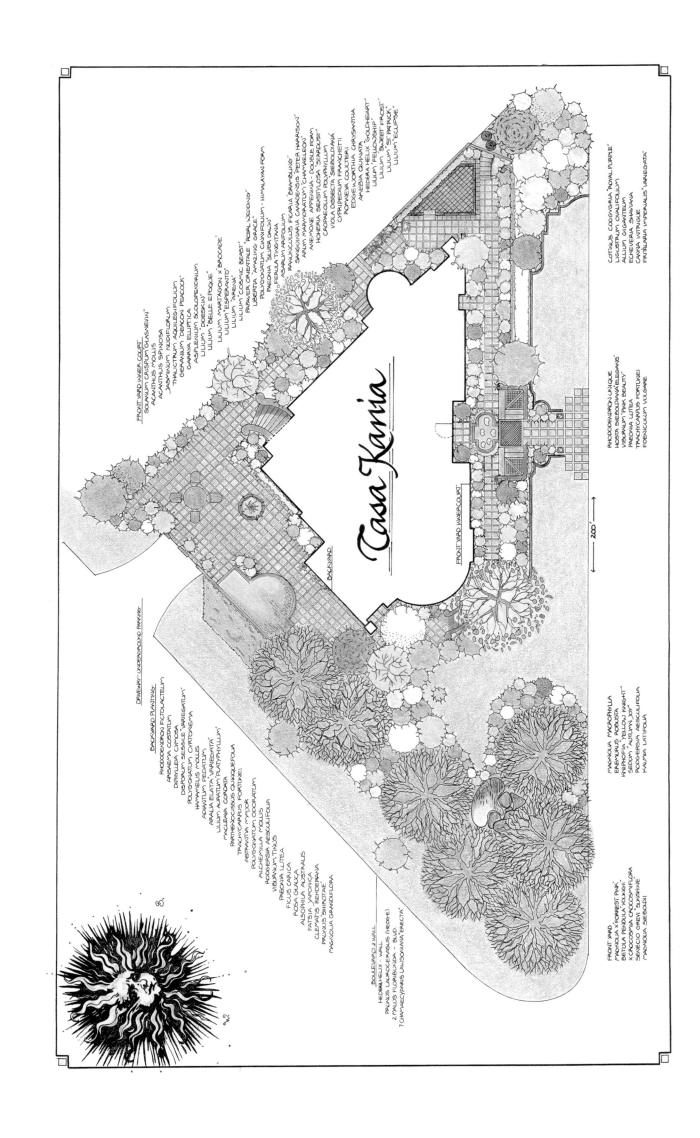

Casa Kania

patina of a pair of copper balls is echoed by drifts of plants with foliage of a similar hue: fleshy rosettes of *Echeveria elegans* like sculpted water lilies, downy mats of lambs' ears (*Stachys byzantina*) and tufts of blue oat grass (*Helictotrichon sempervirens*). Over these hang turk's-cap lilies in redwood shades and the ornate, lime-green and gold flowerheads of *Euphorbia characias* ssp. *wulfenii*. Swords of dusky yucca leaves add exclamation points, and two huge windmill palms slouching against the wall echo the spiky outlines with their own softer sunray pattern.

Rue and lavender continue the blue theme, as does the drooping leathery foliage of a eucalyptus, cleverly sited so that, viewed from straight ahead, it is framed by the terracotta rectangle of chimney rising behind it.

Among the blues and chartreuses, purple plays a subtle counterpoint. *Euphorbia dulcis* 'Chameleon' lives up to its name by starting the season with leaves of deepest plum and progressing by midsummer to a mixture of olive green and a burnt red that matches the turk's-cap lily when it flowers.

At the east end of this border, more purple accents are provided by a smokebush (*Cotinus coggygria* 'Grace'), a black elderberry (*Sambucus nigra* 'Guincho Purple') and the soft feathers of purple fennel.

Once through the gate, the path takes a sharp angle and descends in steps around a small pond planted with papyrus and water lilies. The narrow passage between retaining wall and house is awash in more bold-leaved plants — the purple and orange stripes of *Canna* 'Phaison', the deeply scalloped green of *Acanthus mollis* 'Oak leaf', great dusky spears of *Phormium tenax*, *Eupatorium* 'Diablo' beside a daylily called 'Moonless Night'. A sea-holly (*Eryngium agavifolium*) with leaves like serrated knives holds candelabras of pale green bloom aloft. Lilies are interspersed everywhere,

and around their feet, *Geranium* 'Samobor' mixes the green and black velvet of its leaves with the pale lime flowers of *Primula* 'Francisca'. The lush growth and intensity of colour conjure up an illusion of tropical jungle. All that is missing is a little steam rising off the damp earth.

This finishing touch is provided on the other side of the house, where faint wisps curl up from a small, heated pool tiled in sapphire blue. The shape of the pool and the pattern of soft jade and buff-coloured slates that define its edges reflect a moorish influence that blends well with house and garden. In the dappled shadow of a huge fig tree, the same pattern is repeated on a series of shallow steps that lead up to the house. Each tile in the pattern was painstakingly cut to shape and set in position by Thomas's partner, Brent Beattie (who took a gold medal for the pool design in a Miami competition).

This northern side of the property, facing the water, was reclaimed from a sheer cliff face by the expedient of having a 26-foot retaining wall cast in place. Now trachycarpus palms teeter on its edge, growing happily in the rubble fill topped up with soil, and framing the view over English Bay from the spacious stone-flagged patio. Beside them, a weeping purple beech provides contrast in shape and colour. This secluded garden holds numerous varieties of two of Thomas's favoured plants: magnolias and lilies. As he passes a white *Lilium*

auratum, tall enough to look him in the eye, he pauses to remove its pollen-coated anthers. "A habit from my florist days," he explains. Pollen-stained petals look to him "as though they have been handled by smokers."

Colour themes are subtly repeated throughout this garden in plants of widely differing shape and habit. The white of the *Akebia quinata* and rose framing the front door is continued around the house by the snowy blossoms of 'Mount Fuji' cherries that line the cool, fern-filled corridor beside the house and in the creamy edge on the leaves of *Aralia elata* 'Variegata', whose spiny trunk stands guard over the entrance to the patio. The purple of the beeches is repeated in the leaves of *Lysimachia ciliata*, *Cimicifuga purpurea* and a *Crambe maritima* whose spring foliage is almost black.

Deep peach in the pendant bells of a tall *Brugmansia versicolor* close to the house echoes the soft earth tones of the wall behind it, as do the little flower stalks of echeverias and the taller ones of cape fuchsias (*Phygelius capensis*). The lime trumpets of *Hemerocallis* 'Sweet Potatoes' are edged with apricot, and *Sedum* 'Morchen' marries two themes with its burgundy foliage and burnt sienna flower heads.

Behind a screen of magnolias, underplanted with peonies, a high fence of black railings divides the pool and patio from the more public part of the garden where the two streets meet. Right on the corner, a grove of Lawson cypresses circles a tiny pool, referred to by the owners as "Raccoon Central." To deter these invaders, as well as the human kind, Thomas has planted *Poncirus trifoliata*—"the prickliest plant that I could find"—between the cypress trunks. Although not neglected, this part of the property is rarely visited by the owners, so "zero maintenance" planting is the order of the day. Enjoying its exile here is the only red-flowered plant in the garden—a large clump of *Crocosmia* 'Lucifer'—placed where its blooms can delight passersby while not adding a discordant note to the rest of the garden. G

GLEN PATTERSON'S GARDEN

"I try to follow the Japanese principle of equal proportions of plants, water, rocks and space."

A WILD NATURAL LANDSCAPE of grey crags, icy green waters and towering, wind-torn evergreens surrounds and dominates Glen Patterson's West Vancouver garden, and the garden, like a convex mirror, absorbs these elements, modifies them and reflects them back on a more human scale.

This is a garden of contrasts—of hard, weathered stone and spongy leaf mould, of lofty conifers and minuscule succulents, of rampant vines and neat cushions of azaleas, of sparkling sunshine and deep shadows. And yet it is also a place of harmony, where colours and surfaces blend: a bold shape here is echoed by a subtle one here, the glossy tint of one leaf is matched by the sueded underside of another.

A collector by inclination, Glen Patterson has been greatly influenced in the design of his garden by Jim Nakano, who has worked for and with him in the garden every Sunday for most of the 20 years that it has been in the making.

One of the first modifications to the site by this gardener trained in Zen techniques was also one of the most dramatic. It consisted of peeling off the existing lawn and exposing the skeleton of the wide escarpment that spans most of the property. Now the low bungalow rides on an elephant's back of creased and crannied rock, encrusted with tiny plants and indented here and there with pockets of larger shrubs and perennials. A gnarled mugo pine spreads wide tentacles across one broad plate of rock, while higher up the writhing trunk of a Japanese maple has an equally organic, not to say menacing, appearance. Glen Patterson surveys the result with approval. "Lawns," he says with conviction, "are a dire offense against the environment."

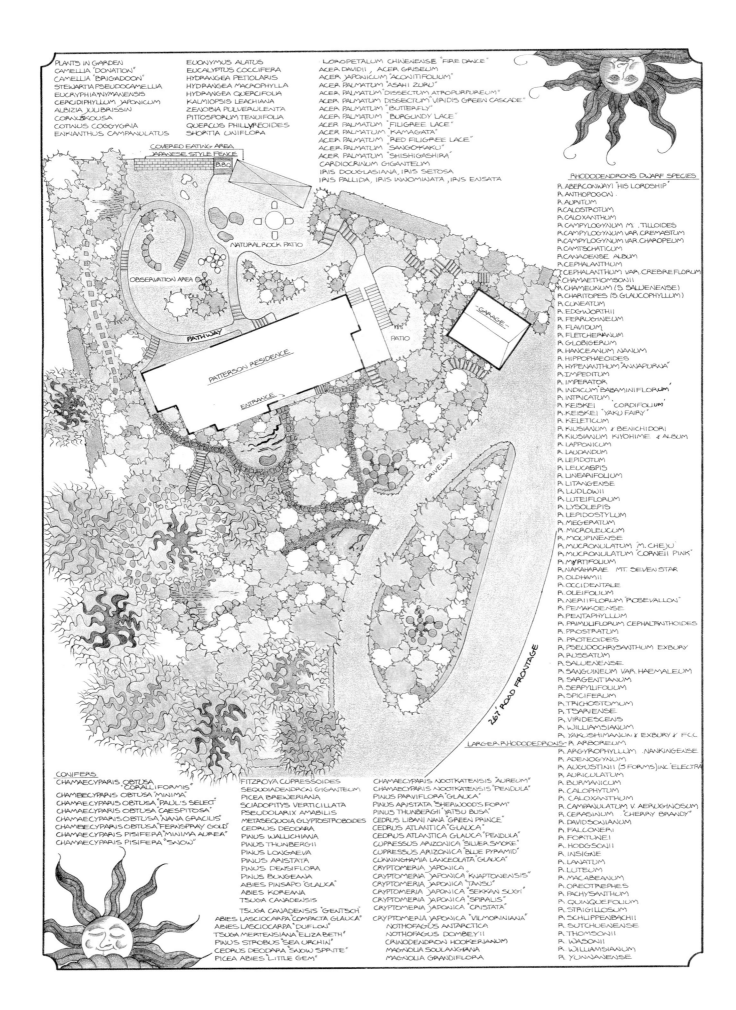

PLANTS IN GARDEN
CAMELLIA "DONATION"
CAMELLIA "BRIGADOON"
STEWARTIA PSEUDOCAMELLIA
EUCRYPHIA "NYMANENSIS"
CERCIDIPHYLLUM JAPONICUM
ALBIZIA JULIBRISSIN
CORNUS KOUSA
COTINUS COGGYGRIA
ENKIANTHUS CAMPANULATUS

EUONYMUS ALATUS
EUCALYPTUS COCCIFERA
HYDRANGEA PETIOLARIS
HYDRANGEA MACROPHYLLA
HYDRANGEA QUERCIFOLIA
KALMIOPSIS LEACHIANA
ZENOBIA PULVERULENTA
PITTOSPORUM TENUIFOLIA
QUERCUS PHILLYREOIDES
SHORTIA UNIFLORA

LOROPETALUM CHINENENSE "FIRE DANCE"
ACER DAVIDII, ACER GRISEUM
ACER JAPONICUM "ACONITIFOLIUM"
ACER PALMATUM "ASAHI ZURU"
ACER PALMATUM DISSECTUM ATROPURPUREUM"
ACER PALMATUM DISSECTUM "VIRIDIS GREEN CASCADE"
ACER PALMATUM "BUTTERFLY"
ACER PALMATUM "BURGUNDY LACE"
ACER PALMATUM "FILIGREE LACE"
ACER PALMATUM "KAMAGATA"
ACER PALMATUM "RED FILIGREE LACE"
ACER PALMATUM "SANGOKAKU"
ACER PALMATUM "SHISHIGASHIRA"
CARDIOCRINUM GIGANTEUM
IRIS DOUGLASIANA, IRIS SETOSA
IRIS PALLIDA, IRIS INNOMINATA, IRIS ENSATA

COVERED EATING AREA
JAPANESE STYLE FENCE
BBQ

NATURAL ROCK PATIO

OBSERVATION AREA

PATHWAY

PATTERSON RESIDENCE

ENTRANCE

PATIO

GARAGE

DRIVEWAY

267' ROAD FRONTAGE

RHODODENDRONS DWARF SPECIES
R. ABERCONWAYI "HIS LORDSHIP"
R. ANTHOPOGON
R. AURITUM
R. CALOSTROTUM
R. CALOXANTHUM
R. CAMPYLOGYNUM M. TILLOIDES
R. CAMPYLOGYNUM VAR. CREMASTUM
R. CAMPYLOGYNUM VAR. CHAROPEUM
R. CAMTSCHATICUM
R. CANADENSE ALBUM
R. CEPHALANTHUM
R. CEPHALANTHUM VAR. CREBREFLORUM
R. CHAMAETHOMSONII
R. CHAMEUNUM (S. SALUENENSE)
R. CHARITOPES (S. GLAUCOPHYLLUM)
R. CUNEATUM
R. EDGWORTHII
R. FERRUGINEUM
R. FLAVIDUM
R. FLETCHERIANUM
R. GLOBIGERUM
R. HANCEANUM NANUM
R. HIPPOPHAEOIDES
R. HYPENANTHUM "ANNAPURNA"
R. IMPEDITUM
R. IMPERATOR
R. INDICUM BALSAMINIFLORUM
R. INTRICATUM
R. KEISKEI "CORDIFOLIUM"
R. KEISKEI "YAKU FAIRY"
R. KELETICUM
R. KIUSIANUM x BENICHIDORI
R. KIUSIANUM KIYOHIME x ALBUM
R. LAPPONICUM
R. LADDANUM
R. LEPIDOTUM
R. LEUCASPIS
R. LINEARIFOLIUM
R. LITANGENSE
R. LUDLOWII
R. LUTEIFLORUM
R. LYSOLEPIS
R. LEPIDOSTYLUM
R. MEGERATUM
R. MICROLEUCUM
R. MOUPINENSE
R. MUCRONULATUM "M. CHEJU"
R. MUCRONULATUM "CORNEII PINK"
R. MYRTIFOLIUM
R. NAKAHARAE "MT. SEVEN STAR"
R. OLDHAMII
R. OCCIDENTALE
R. OLEIFOLIUM
R. NERIIFLORUM "ROSEVALLON"
R. PEMAKOENSE
R. PENTAPHYLLUM
R. PRIMULIFLORUM CEPHALANTHOIDES
R. PROSTRATUM
R. PROTEOIDES
R. PSEUDOCHRYSANTHUM EXBURY
R. RUSSATUM
R. SALUENENSE
R. SANGUINEUM VAR. HAEMALEUM
R. SARGENTIANUM
R. SERPYLLIFOLIUM
R. SPICIFERUM
R. TRICHOSTOMUM
R. TSARIENSE
R. VIRIDESCENS
R. WILLIAMSIANUM
R. YAKUSHIMANUM x EXBURY x FCC

LARGER RHODODENDRONS
R. ARBOREUM
R. ARGYROPHYLLUM NANKINGENSE
R. ADENOGYNUM
R. AUGUSTINII (3 FORMS) INC. "ELECTRA"
R. AURICULATUM
R. BURMANICUM
R. CALOPHYTUM
R. CALOXANTHUM
R. CAMPANULATUM V. AERUGINOSUM
R. CERASINUM "CHERRY BRANDY"
R. DAVIDSONIANUM
R. FALCONERI
R. FORTUNEI
R. HODGSONII
R. INSIGNE
R. LANATUM
R. LUTEUM
R. MACABEANUM
R. OREOTREPHES
R. PACHYSANTHUM
R. QUINQUEFOLIUM
R. STRIGILLOSUM
R. SCHLIPPENBACHII
R. SUTCHUENENSE
R. THOMSONII
R. WASONII
R. WILLIAMSIANUM
R. YUNNANENSE

CONIFERS
CHAMAECYPARIS OBTUSA "CORALLIFORMIS"
CHAMAECYPARIS OBTUSA "MINIMA"
CHAMAECYPARIS OBTUSA "PAUL'S SELECT"
CHAMAECYPARIS OBTUSA "CAESPITOSA"
CHAMAECYPARIS OBTUSA "NANA GRACILIS"
CHAMAECYPARIS OBTUSA "FERNSPRAY GOLD"
CHAMAECYPARIS PISIFERA "MINIMA AUREA"
CHAMAECYPARIS PISIFERA "SNOW"

FITZROYA CUPRESSOIDES
SEQUOIADENDRON GIGANTEUM
PICEA BREWERIANA
SCIADOPITYS VERTICILLATA
PSEUDOLARIX AMABILIS
METASEQUOIA GLYPTOSTROBOIDES
CEDRUS DEODARA
PINUS WALLICHIANA
PINUS THUNBERGII
PINUS LONGAEVA
PINUS ARISTATA
PINUS DENSIFLORA
PINUS BUNGEANA
ABIES PINSAPO "GLAUCA"
ABIES KOREANA
TSUGA CANADENSIS
TSUGA CANADENSIS "GENTSCH"
ABIES LASIOCARPA "COMPACTA GLAUCA"
ABIES LASIOCARPA "DUFLON"
TSUGA MERTENSIANA "ELIZABETH"
PINUS STROBUS "SEA URCHIN"
CEDRUS DEODARA "SNOW SPRITE"
PICEA ABIES "LITTLE GEM"

CHAMAECYPARIS NOOTKATENSIS "AUREUM"
CHAMAECYPARIS NOOTKATENSIS "PENDULA"
PINUS PARVIFLORA "GLAUCA"
PINUS ARISTATA "SHERWOOD'S FORM"
PINUS THUNBERGII "YATSU BUSA"
CEDRUS LIBANI NANA "GREEN PRINCE"
CEDRUS ATLANTICA "GLAUCA"
CEDRUS ATLANTICA GLAUCA "PENDULA"
CUPRESSUS ARIZONICA "SILVER SMOKE"
CUPRESSUS ARIZONICA "BLUE PYRAMID"
CUNNINGHAMIA LANCEOLATA "GLAUCA"
CRYPTOMERIA JAPONICA
CRYPTOMERIA JAPONICA "KNAPTONENSIS"
CRYPTOMERIA JAPONICA "TANSU"
CRYPTOMERIA JAPONICA "SEKKAN SUGI"
CRYPTOMERIA JAPONICA "SPIRALIS"
CRYPTOMERIA JAPONICA "CRISTATA"
CRYPTOMERIA JAPONICA "VILMORINIANA"
NOTHOFAGUS ANTARCTICA
NOTHOFAGUS DOMBEYII
CRINODENDRON HOOKERIANUM
MAGNOLIA SOULANGIANA
MAGNOLIA GRANDIFLORA

Behind the house, another, steeper crag rises sharply to a summit well above the roofline. From this crow's-nest, a panoramic view encompasses Lighthouse Park, the Gulf of Georgia and, far to the southeast, the towers of the city. On the highest point of land, a fir—clipped to emulate the ragged outlines of its taller neighbours—keeps company with a pair of *Cupressus glabra* 'Silver Smoke' and the shining wands of *Rubus thibetanus*.

A laurel hedge used to run along the edge of the property here, screening it from the house behind. This "curse of the English," as Glen Patterson describes it, has been replaced by a Japanese-influenced fence. Close by, a shelter for alfresco dining echoes the same archi-

tectural elements in its elegant roof and supporting poles. The plateau it occupies is bounded by a low box hedge—not the usual solid green wall but clipped to reveal snaking white stems beneath the foliage, and looking extraordinarily like a row of miniature mangroves.

Descent from the pinnacle is directly down the rock face for the adventurous, or by a narrow set of stone steps for the faint of heart. The ledge on which the house sits is wide enough to allow for a small patio, and on this rare level surface Glen Patterson has set a collection of fascinating specimens in pots: the spiny green and white rosettes of *Carlina acaulis*, several slate-blue echeveria and one dusky plum-coloured one called 'Black Knight'; *Aeonium* 'Zwartkop' like a shiny black rosette; and two Japanese maples, *Acer japonicum* 'Koto-no-ito' (in translation "old harp with fine strings," which neatly describes the fineness of their foliage).

The patio overlooks a garage, enveloped in clematis and a beautiful purple-leaved grape, and is screened from the road below by a massive kiwi vine, which Glen is often tempted to take down, but has so far spared for its annual bounty of fruit. Paths, interspersed by steps where the terrain is steep, wind from the patio in a number of directions. One zigzags down to the road, passing clusters of small bulbs in spring, and the taller spires of species gladiolus (*G. papilio*), hung with bells of green-tinged violet in summer. Another leads to the front door, passing under an arch of *Dicentra scandens*, a climbing variety of bleeding heart with yellow flowers like flocks of tiny canaries.

The steepness of the terrain creates a bank on the high side of each descending path, which allows for close

dendrons value more highly than the flowers. Most often a cinnamon brown, in this instance it resembles fine white velvet.

Here also is a collection of *Cryptomeria*, high on Glen's list of worthy species because they not only contribute a glow of autumn colour to the garden but also lend themselves so well to shaping. Lurking beneath are arisaemas with leaves like giant clovers and flowers like cobras, bronze-leaved saxifrages and the round, heavily textured foliage of a *Shortia uniflora*, a native of Japan, which bears pink flowers in spring and has blanketed the ground to an extent that draws envy from visiting plant aficionados.

At the far end of this calm well of green shade, steps awash in the shiny foliage of begonias lead upwards past lilies, an oakleaf hydrangea and the creased trunk of an old cherry draped in tendrils of chocolate vine (*Akebia quinata*). Highlights of pale jade in the foliage of a *Rhododendron oreotrephes* and the reptilian trunk of a maple (*Acer davidii*) stand out among the richer greens that surround them. At the top of the steps, a path leads around the side of the house to a recently renovated nook at the base of the high crag that fills the back of the property. Here, in what used to be a composting corner, a small pool is taking shape. The rock face that rises above it is pitted with crevices where sedums, sempervivums, and the tiny pink and white daisies of *Erigeron karvinskianus* thrive, apparently without any sustaining soil. Two cranberry-coloured smokebushes cling precariously to a shallow ledge. The choice of route is now to scale the cliff again for another look at the vista across the rooftop, or to skirt the house and descend over the front shelves of rock toward the road. Either way, there is the broad sweep of west coast landscape to admire, and a guarantee of unusual plants on either side to re-focus attention on close-up detail. ଓ

inspection of the many treasures Glen has collected from near and far, some of them tiny versions of plants more familiar in their larger forms. Fat red teardrops hang from a *Crinodendron hookerianum* and a *Rhododendron quinqefolium* displays leaves like five-pointed stars edged in dull crimson. Rhododendrons are Glen's specialty, and many of the dwarf varieties are here, close to eye-level, so that their felted foliage and tiny flowers will not escape notice.

Where the ground levels out at the foot of the massive outcropping, a golden full-moon maple stands beneath the dark trunks of conifers, its chartreuse foliage a beacon signalling a change in mood as paths converge to dive beneath a canopy of lacy foliage, over which loom the giant firs and cedars of the west coast forest. The shadows deepen and the ground on either side becomes more mossy. Rough stepping stones lead to a quiet woodland pool surrounded by *Meconopsis betonicifolia*, ferns like splayed green fingers, drifts of candelabra primulas, tall spears of iris and clumps of bold-leaved *Rodgersia aesculifolia* and *Darmera peltata*. More azaleas and rhododendrons inhabit this shady microclimate, including a beautiful *Rhododendron tsariense*, its dark green leaves undercoated with indumentum, the soft suede-like finish that connoisseurs of rhodo-

PAGE 148
Still water reflects blue Siberian irises and a skillfully pruned
Chamaecyparis pisifera 'Filifera Aurea'.

PAGE 149
The crimson teardrops of *Crinodendron hookerianum*.

PAGE 151
Lichen patterns a boulder beside a runnel of water.

PAGE 152
Pruning enhances the shape of a juniper.

PAGE 153
The surrounding west coast lanscape lends its own beauty to the
garden.

BILL WALTER'S GARDEN

"The garden is layered, just as the house is layered.
Even the footing of the fence is designed to echo the angle of the roof."

FROM THE EDGE OF THE curb to the back wall of the property and beyond, everything is in keeping with the Japanese theme. The traditional grass that lines the boulevards of streets in this part of old Shaughnessy has been replaced with a sea of rounded grey pebbles and small-scale outcroppings of black lava rock fringed with moss and succulents. The low garage that faces the street supports on its flat roof a similar but larger lava rock and a small pine enclosed by a simple railing of heavy bamboo beams. To right and left, rough slabs of granite climb through a mossy landscape of Japanese maples, small rhododendrons and azaleas, prostrate junipers and winter-flowering heather to curve around the sides of the low-slung, angular house, one of a few in Vancouver that show the influence of Frank Lloyd Wright.

Striking as the design is from this aspect, it hardly prepares you for the drama of the garden behind the house. Making a virtue of the steeply sloping, half-acre lot, Bill Walter and landscape architect Brian Clarke have sculpted the terrain into a series of levels, dominated by huge granite rocks, carefully placed specimen trees and a traditional tea-house. From the highest point at the southwest corner, a waterfall tumbles over a huge block of rough granite into a limpid pool where carp draw slow. red-gold arabesques beneath the surface. Two separate streams flow out from this point, one rushing, one trickling down toward a sliver of a channel that borders a slate-paved terrace along the back of the house. Look

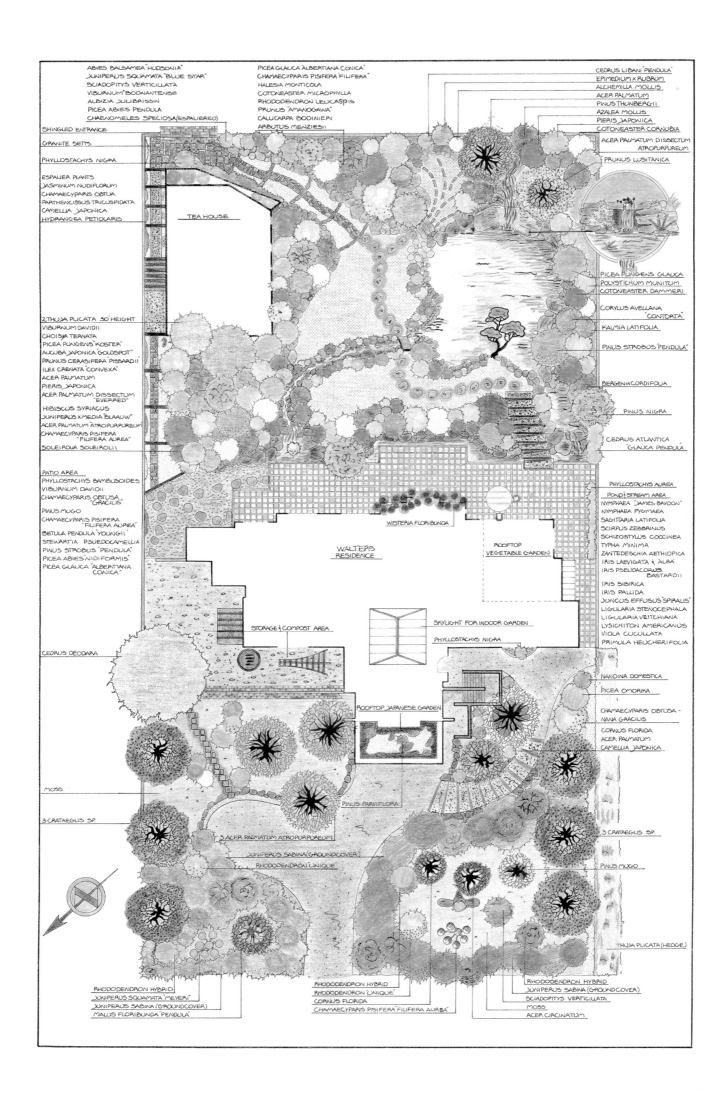

ABIES BALSAMEA "HUDSONIA"
JUNIPERUS SQUAMATA "BLUE STAR"
SCIADOPITYS VERTICILLATA
VIBURNUM BODNANTENSE
ALBIZIA JULIBRISSIN
PICEA ABIES PENDULA
CHAENOMELES SPECIOSA (ESPALIERED)

PICEA GLAUCA "ALBERTIANA CONICA"
CHAMAECYPARIS PISIFERA "FILIFERA"
HALESIA MONTICOLA
COTONEASTER MICROPHYLLA
RHODODENDRON LEUCASPIS
PRUNUS "AMANOGAWA"
CALLICARPA BODINIERI
ARBUTUS MENZIESII

CEDRUS LIBANI "PENDULA"
EPIMEDIUM X RUBRUM
ALCHEMILLA MOLLIS
ACER PALMATUM
PINUS THUNBERGII
AZALEA MOLLIS
PIERIS JAPONICA
COTONEASTER CORNUBIA

SHINGLED ENTRANCE

ACER PALMATUM DISSECTUM
ATROPURPUREUM

GRANITE SETTS

PRUNUS LUSITANICA

PHYLLOSTACHYS NIGRA

ESPALIER PLANTS
JASMINUM NUDIFLORUM
CHAMAECYPARIS OBTUA
PARTHENCISSUS TRICUSPIDATA
CAMELLIA JAPONICA
HYDRANGEA PETIOLARIS

TEA HOUSE

PICEA PUNGENS GLAUCA
POLYSTICHUM MUNITUM
COTONEASTER DAMMERI

CORYLUS AVELLANA
"CONTORTA"

2 THUJA PLICATA 30' HEIGHT
VIBURNUM DAVIDII
CHOISYA TERNATA
PICEA PUNGENS "KOSTER"
AUCUBA JAPONICA "GOLDSPOT"
PRUNUS CERASIFERA PISSARDII
ILEX CRENATA "CONVEXA"
ACER PALMATUM
PIERIS JAPONICA
ACER PALMATUM DISSECTUM
"EVERRED"
HIBISCUS SYRIACUS
JUNIPERUS X MEDIA "BLAAUW"
ACER PALMATUM "ATROPURPUREUM"
CHAMAECYPARIS PISIFERA
"FILIFERA AUREA"
SOLEIROLIA SOLEIROLII

KALMIA LATIFOLIA

PINUS STROBUS "PENDULA"

BERGENIA CORDIFOLIA

PINUS NIGRA

CEDRUS ATLANTICA
"GLAUCA PENDULA"

PATIO AREA
PHYLLOSTACHYS BAMBUSOIDES
VIBURNUM DAVIDII
CHAMAECYPARIS OBTUSA
"GRACILIS"
PINUS MUGO
CHAMAECYPARIS PISIFERA
"FILIFERA AUREA"
BETULA PENDULA "YOUNGII"
STEWARTIA PSUEDOCAMELLIA
PINUS STROBUS "PENDULA"
PICEA ABIES "NIDIFORMIS"
PICEA GLAUCA "ALBERTIANA
CONICA"

WISTERIA FLORIBUNDA

WALTERS
RESIDENCE

ROOFTOP
VEGETABLE GARDEN

PHYLLOSTACHYS AUREA
POND & STREAM AREA
NYMPHAEA "JAMES BRYDON"
NYMPHAEA PYGMAEA
SAGITTARIA LATIFOLIA
SCIRPUS ZEBRINUS
SCHIZOSTYLIS COCCINEA
TYPHA MINIMA
ZANTEDESCHIA AETHIOPICA
IRIS LAEVIGATA & "ALBA"
IRIS PSEUDACORUS
BASTARDII
IRIS SIBIRICA
IRIS PALLIDA
JUNCUS EFFUSUS "SPIRALIS"
LIGULARIA STENOCEPHALA
LIGULARIA VEITCHIANA
LYSICHITON AMERICANUS
VIOLA CUCULLATA
PRIMULA HEUCHERIFOLIA

STORAGE & COMPOST AREA

SKYLIGHT FOR INDOOR GARDEN

PHYLLOSTACHYS NIGRA

CEDRUS DEODARA

NANDINA DOMESTICA

PICEA OMORIKA

ROOFTOP JAPANESE GARDEN

CHAMAECYPARIS OBTUSA
NANA GRACILIS

CORNUS FLORIDA
ACER PALMATUM
CAMELLIA JAPONICA

MOSS

PINUS PARVIFLORA

3 CRATAEGUS SP.

3 CRATAEGUS SP.

3 ACER PALMATUM ATROPURPUREUM

JUNIPERUS SABINA (GROUNDCOVER)

PINUS MUGO

RHODODENDRON "UNIQUE"

THUJA PLICATA (HEDGE)

RHODODENDRON HYBRID
JUNIPERUS SQUAMATA "MEYERI"
JUNIPERUS SABINA (GROUNDCOVER)
MALUS FLORIBUNDA "PENDULA"

RHODODENDRON HYBRID
RHODODENDRON "UNIQUE"
CORNUS FLORIDA
CHAMAECYPARIS PISIFERA FILIFERA AUREA

RHODODENDRON HYBRID
JUNIPERUS SABINA (GROUNDCOVER)
SCIADOPITYS VERTICILLATA
MOSS
ACER CIRCINATUM

"This is a yard on a north-facing hill — a place of shadows."

deep into the dark water of the channel and you can see the shadowy movement of trout. The narrowness of the watercourse and a low barricade of thick bamboo protect them from marauding herons, but not from an occasional fishing foray by Bill Walter. Against the glass wall of the house behind, a wide-spreading wisteria with a massive trunk softens the sharp angles of the eaves.

In a mere seven years, the owner and his architect have transformed this garden from an eroded, water-sodden hillside into a startling vision. Earth was scooped out to create the levels, and rubberized filter cloth was laid in the excavations for the water features. Two giant cranes hoisted chunks of Pitt River granite, the largest weighing 18.65 tonnes, over hydro wires along the

southern boundary and manoeuvred them into place on the site. Then Bill began to collect and plant the bamboos, shrubs and vines that flourish alongside the watercourses and small platforms of grass or Corsican mint that define the different levels of the garden.

It is a garden in perpetual motion. Leaves flicker in the lightest of breezes, and everywhere water cascades, glides or drips as it seeks its level. Even the eaves troughs on the house channel the run-off not into downpipes, but over sturdy chains descending deep into the core of carefully positioned chunks of black lava rock. When it rains, to be in this garden is like being at the bottom of a waterfall.

By contrast with the fluctuating light and shadow of

moving water, colours are subtle. The rocks and much of the foliage blend with the blue-grey walls of the house. Touches of russet, and a flick of brightness here and there in the flowers of a bergenia or a rhododendron are like bright threads woven into a sombre tapestry. A tiny clump of cyclamen emerging from a mossy pocket glows pink on emerald green, a carpet of *Euonymus fortunei* 'Emerald 'n' Gold' sparkles under the umbrella of a Camperdown elm, a weeping copper beech traces the line of rocks behind the carp pool with burnished leaves that blend into the trunk of an arbutus tree coming up behind.

"It's a classic Momoyama Period Japanese garden," says Brian Clarke. "A circle within a circle, largely monochrome, layered, textured."

This concept of concentric circles neatly extends to the way such a stylized Oriental garden can lie hidden in the heart of Vancouver's most English neighbourhood, while holding unseen at its own centre yet another small world. A vegetable plot, reached by a discreet flight of stairs, occupies the flat roof of the house and, with its raised beds of treated lumber, trellises of grapes, kiwi vine, and 'Dragon's Tongue' beans, and row of columnar apple trees, owes more to the French tradition of the "potager" than to England or Japan.

To occupy the high, sheltered corner of the property where vegetables once grew, Brian Clarke designed a Japanese teahouse with elegant vertical windows carefully positioned to frame views of the landscape "like colour postcards." He is also responsible for the heavy gates of English elm set into the wall behind the teahouse — so much at home in their Oriental setting but in fact salvaged from the old Timber Club at the Hotel Vancouver.

From these gates a sweeping S-curve of Nelson Island granite slabs delineates the route by which 40 truckloads of dirt were removed from the original hillside. The slabs are recycled, too; flame-finished on all sides, they were destined for landfill before Brian Clarke rescued them from a demolition site. Now their weight and substance provide a counterbalance to the quicksilver arc of water on the other side of the garden, as well as a firm footing for the transport in and out of a cavalcade of plants. A dying maple recently went out that way, and was replaced by a seven-metre Serbian spruce lowered over the wall into the vacated spot, where it now rises like a compass needle above the horizontal line of the steel grey wall.

Even outside the wall, the theme is continued along the street that runs behind the property, with simple groups of shrubs planted between long stretches of gravel. Passersby, intrigued by this careful composition, might wonder what lies within. More, as it happens, than they are likely to imagine.. ☙

DON ARMSTRONG'S GARDEN

"I'm a plunker — nothing in this yard was composed.
There are no favourite plants."

There is also no lawn — not the vestige of a blade of grass except for ornamental varieties, and there are plenty of those. This is a garden in which the rare, the vaguely recognizable and the downright familiar alternately delight the eye and tax the memory bank.

Don Armstrong counts 30 different kinds of trilliums, 27 species of arisaemas and seven assorted daphnes among his plants. And that's just for starters. Ferns, succulents, clematis, lilies, evening primroses, dwarf firs . . . the list could go on forever.

Known for years in its Kerrisdale neighbourhood as "the pink house," this modest dwelling has recently received a more conservative coat of light and dark olive green which Don has not quite come to terms with. Nonetheless it sits easily among the different levels of the garden whose contours provide more areas for Don

to plant than the flat surface of a standard lot.

Like the quarry garden in Queen Elizabeth Park, this garden has turned an apparent liability into an asset. In this case, it was the hole left following the removal of a backyard swimming pool that gave the land its unusual vertical dimension. Now filled with plants, small ponds, boulders of various sizes and an occasional sculpture, the former pool is the focus for a garden where only the path that links front and back yards still holds to its original level. Small trails radiating off this main access wind in all directions, leading the visitor to discover the many treasures squirrelled away in unexpected corners. There are the arisaemas, like little dragons' heads rearing out of the soil, a peony with seed heads like mediaeval jesters' caps, a true evening primrose (*Oenothera sp.*), dwarf conifers with

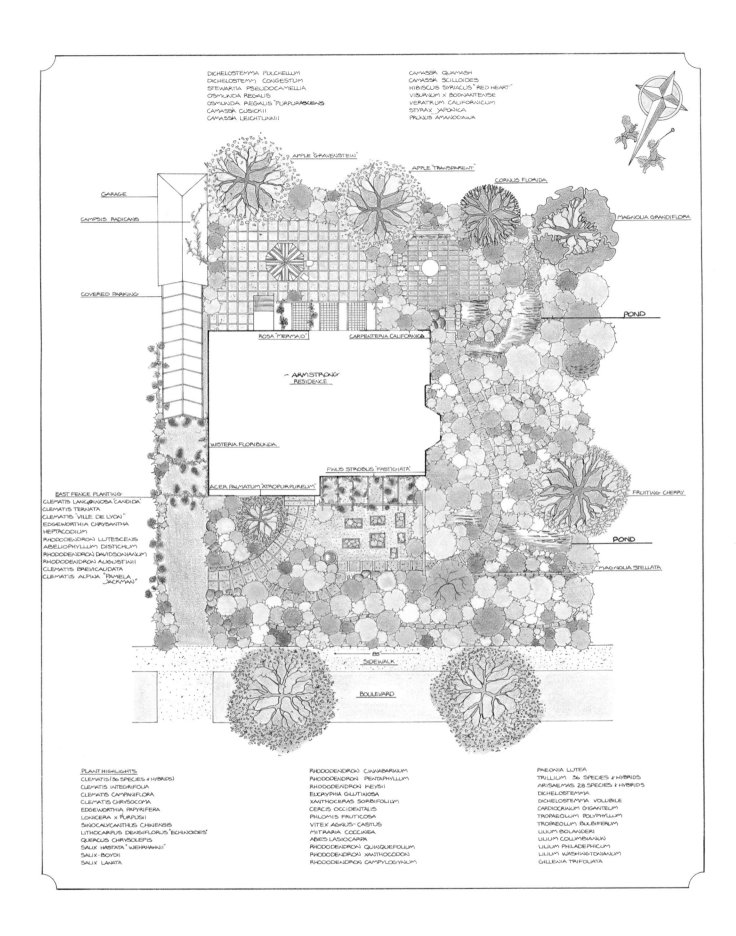

blue needles like the bristles of a hairbrush, sagebrush from the Okanagan and a 'Mermaid' rose, whose single yellow flowers nod down from the back porch, basking in the heat trap of a south-facing patio and "growing in soil that is practically straight sand," according to Don.

Beside the small paved patio, a quartet of flute-playing cherubs painted ox-blood red provides silent accompaniment to alfresco meals. They lend a certain air of whimsy to their surroundings, although more than one visitor has looked askance at them. Around their feet,

fronds of blue and white willow gentian bloom between green clumps of hosta and hellebores. Don points out a trillium relative, *Paris polyphylla,* whose sterile flowers look like daddy-long-legs with blue and khaki legs; a blue urn placed nearby picks up the colour theme. On the other side of the patio, right on the corner of the house, a chaste tree (*Vitex agnus-castus*) reflects more blue when its flowers open in September.

One step down from the patio, another small platform provides space for a sturdy bench laden with pots

with rough boulders. On the steepest corner, lilacs and tall-growing perennials like phlox and Japanese anemones abut the fence. As the ground levels out to where the driveway runs along the eastern side, pockets between the rocks are bright with tiny bulbs and tulips in spring, followed later in the season by crimson verbena, pink and lavender petunias, and the grass-green leaves and fluted vermilion flowers of *Zauschneria californica.*

A narrow path winds from the driveway to the front door, where zinc buckets of orange begonias sit on the porch steps. A purple wisteria climbs beside the porch and rambles across a pergola over the remaining facade. In its shadow, lilies surround a display of trough gardens, dripping with tiny sedums and saxifrages. Some of these came from the garden of a kindred spirit, Thelma Chapman, who bequeathed to Don her plant collection, including 200 rhododendrons.

Alongside the driveway, many of the shrubs and vines were chosen for special interest, particularly fragrance. Wintersweet (*Chimonanthus praecox*) blooms early in the new year beside a richly scented shrubby honeysuckle (*Lonicera × purpusia*) and a *Heptacodium,* which Don confirms has a "definite jasmine scent." Early rhododendrons flank the side fence, entwined with a *Tropaeolum speciosum* whose little red flowers swim like goldfish across their dark foliage in summer. A vigorous *Clematis cirrhosa balearica,* often called the fern-leaf clematis because of its finely cut evergreen leaves, appears to be springing straight out of the blacktop against the wall of the house to cover an arbour that spans the approach to the garage. If the sun is strong enough to warm the wall, its small ivory bells begin to open in January.

of plants that Don has raised from seed but not yet inserted into the fabric of the garden. Young arisaemas, trilliums and dwarf conifers sprout here in the shelter of a climbing hydrangea that is making its way along the backyard fence. Where he will find room to fit them in is anybody's guess, as every inch of ground seems already occupied, including the risers between stone steps where tufts of greenery brush against your shoes as you pass. Even the four ponds are thick with water lily pads, iris and whorls of giant horsetail. A tiny watercourse remains clear, trickling between lava rocks into a pool where pitcher plants wade out towards a moss-covered islet, and a clutch of bronze Chinese ducks quack silently on the brink. Above, the land rises to a high crest on one back corner where a glossy *Magnolia grandiflora* presides over the teeming cavalcade of plant life. One ledge below, the feathery shape of a huge tree peony is the first thing to catch your eye. Closer inspection reveals that the vertical faces of rock around it are encrusted with many kinds of sedums.

The private garden, enclosed on all sides, is screened from the sidewalk by a discreet lattice fence. Because the property is on a slope, Don has been able to scallop the "public" garden outside the fence into terraces edged

The garage itself is swamped in a mass of *Campsis radicans*, the hummingbird vine, which also swarms the high fence of split cedar that runs between garage and house, blocking off the private back garden from public view. In midsummer, its flame-coloured trumpets claim attention from both sides of the fence.

Entering through the gate in this fence, you are again on the sunny patio. Make another round of the garden and an entirely different selection of plants will attract your attention. Retrace your steps and new details will spring into focus, as if you have turned the cylinder of a kaleidoscope and the pieces have shifted into a new pattern. It may be the purple bark on a manzanita peeling back to show a skin of chartreuse beneath, or the pale green snakeheads of a clump of allium. If Don hasn't ousted it, you may even catch sight of "the ugliest plant in the garden"—a double-flowered tiger lily. ୧

PAGE 160
Dense planting is accented with quirky ornamental touches.

PAGE 161
The striking leaves of a Pelargonium.

PAGE 163
The former swimming pool is now awash with plants.

PAGE 164
Cherubs greet the flowering of a *Cardiocrinum giganteum*.

PAGE 165
A spring composition of pansies and species tulips (*Tulipa clusiana chrysantha*).

JANET WOOD'S GARDEN

"I didn't want a private garden. I wanted people passing by to be able to look in and enjoy it."

WHEN JANET WOOD RETURNED to Vancouver after five years of living on Vancouver Island, she had some difficulty finding the right place to live. When her realtor doubtfully suggested a recent listing in Southlands, an area familiar to most Vancouver residents for horses and golf courses, she agreed to take a look. With the surrounding ditch as high as the land, the property was little more than a swamp enclosed by hedges of laurel and pyramid cedars. Nevertheless, in Janet's eyes it had one great virtue. "I knew as soon as I saw the first sign advertising free manure that it was the right place for me."

Fourteen years later, the stables across the street continue to make regular contributions to her flourishing garden, and riders passing by are rewarded by the colour and fragrance that comes from over 300 roses that are the mainstay of her garden.

Draining the land and raising the soil level became her first priority, followed by removal of the hedges. "They weren't neighbourly," she says. "And besides, they blocked the light and interfered with good air circulation."

Her interest in roses had begun more or less on a whim five years before she moved to her present location. "I didn't know one rose from another," she recalls. "I bought a little soft-cover book on rose-growing, and after reading it I thought 'I'll never be able to do this.'" Nevertheless, on the advice of a friend she ordered her first five plants.

By the time she bought the Southlands property, she already knew that she wanted more uprights than fences

Janet Wood's Rose Garden

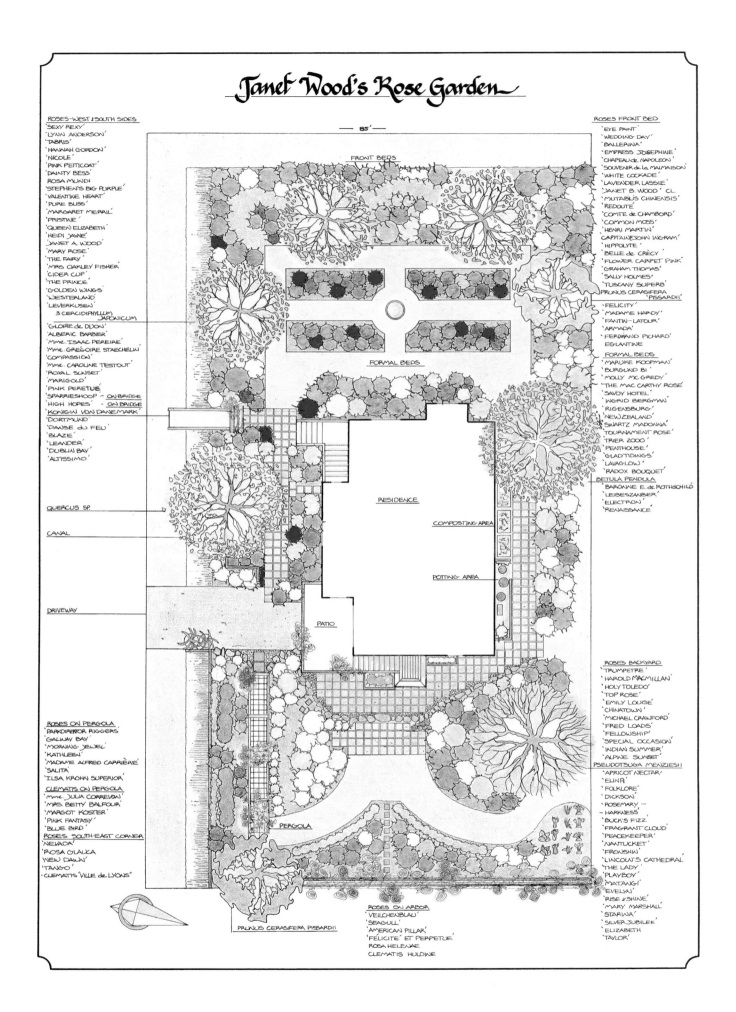

85'

ROSES-WEST & SOUTH SIDES
'SEXY REXY'
'LYNN ANDERSON'
'TABRIS'
'HANNAH GORDON'
'NICOLE'
'PINK PETTICOAT'
'DAINTY BESS'
ROSA MUNDI
'STEPHEN'S BIG PURPLE'
'VALENTINE HEART'
'PURE BLISS'
'MARGARET MERRIL'
'PRISTINE'
'QUEEN ELIZABETH'
'HEIDI JAYNE'
'JANET A. WOOD'
'MARY ROSE'
'THE FAIRY'
'MRS. OAKLEY FISHER'
'CIDER CUP'
'THE PRINCE'
'GOLDEN WINGS'
'WESTERLAND'
'LEVERKUSEN'
3 CERCIDIPHYLLUM JAPONICUM
'GLOIRE de DIJON'
'ALBERIC BARBIER'
'MME. ISAAC PEREIRE'
'MME. GREGOIRE STAECHELIN'
'COMPASSION'
'MME. CAROLINE TESTOUT'
'ROYAL SUNSET'
'MARIGOLD'
'PINK PERPETUE'
'SPARRIESHOOP' — ON BRIDGE
'HIGH HOPES' — ON BRIDGE
'KONIGIN VON DANEMARK'
'DORTMUND'
'DANSE du FEU'
'BLAZE'
'LEANDER'
'DUBLIN BAY'
'ALTISSIMO'

QUERCUS SP.

CANAL

DRIVEWAY

ROSES ON PERGOLA
'PAROL/ANTOR RIGGERS'
'GALWAY BAY'
'MORNING JEWEL'
'KATHLEEN'
'MADAME ALFRED CARRIÈRE'
'SALITA'
'ILSA KROHN SUPERIOR'
CLEMATIS ON PERGOLA
'MME. JULIA CORREVON'
'MRS. BETTY BALFOUR'
'MARGOT KOSTER'
'PINK FANTASY'
'BLUE BIRD'
ROSES SOUTH-EAST CORNER
'NEVADA'
'ROSA GLAUCA'
'NEW DAWN'
'TANGO'
'CLEMATIS 'VILLE de LYONS''

ROSES FRONT BED
'EYE PAINT'
'WEDDING DAY'
'BALLERINA'
'EMPRESS JOSEPHINE'
'CHAPEAU de NAPOLEON'
'SOUVENIR de la MALMAISON'
'WHITE COCKADE'
'LAVENDER LASSIE'
'JANET B. WOOD' CL
'MUTABILIS CHINENSIS'
'REDOUTE'
'COMTE de CHAMBORD'
'COMMON MOSS'
'HENRI MARTIN'
'CAPITAINE JOHN INGRAM'
'HIPPOLYTE'
'BELLE de CRÈCY'
'FLOWER CARPET PINK'
'GRAHAM THOMAS'
'SALLY HOLMES'
'TUSCANY SUPERB'
PRUNUS CERASIFERA 'PISSARDII'
'FELICITY'
'MADAME HARDY'
'FANTIN-LATOUR'
'ARMADA'
'FERDINAND PICHARD'
'EGLANTINE'
FORMAL BEDS
'MARIJKE KOOPMAN'
'BURGUND 81'
'MOLLY MC GREDY'
'THE MAC CARTHY ROSE'
'SAVOY HOTEL'
'INGRID BERGMAN'
'RIGENSBURG'
'NEW ZEALAND'
'SWARTZ MADONNA'
'TOURNAMENT ROSE'
'TRIER 2000'
'PENTHOUSE'
'GLAD TIDINGS'
'LAVAGLOW'
'RADOX BOUQUET'
BETULA PENDULA
'BARONNE E. de ROTHSCHILD'
'LIEBESZANBER'
'ELECTRON'
'RENAISSANCE'

FRONT BEDS

FORMAL BEDS

RESIDENCE

COMPOSTING AREA

POTTING AREA

PATIO

ROSES BACKYARD
'TRUMPETRE'
'HAROLD MACMILLAN'
'HOLY TOLEDO'
'TOP ROSE'
'EMILY LOUISE'
'CHINATOWN'
'MICHAEL CRAWFORD'
'FRED LOADS'
'FELLOWSHIP'
'SPECIAL OCCASION'
'INDIAN SUMMER'
'ALPINE SUNSET'
PSEUDOTSUGA MENZIESII
'APRICOT NECTAR'
'ELINA'
'FOLKLORE'
'DICKSON'
'ROSEMARY — HARKNESS'
'BUCK'S FIZZ'
'FRAGRANT CLOUD'
'PEACEKEEPER'
'NANTUCKET'
'FROJSHIN'
'LINCOLN'S CATHEDRAL'
'THE LADY'
'PLAYBOY'
'MATANGI'
'EVELYN'
'RISE & SHINE'
'MARY MARSHALL'
'STARINA'
'SILVER JUBILEE'
'ELIZABETH TAYLOR'

PERGOLA

ROSES ON ARBOR
'VEILCHENBLAU'
'SEAGULL'
'AMERICAN PILLAR'
'FÉLICITÉ' ET PERPETUE'
ROSA HELENAE
CLEMATIS HULDINE

PRUNUS CERASIFERA PISSARDII

"I don't have favourites. I think, 'That was beautiful this year',
but then I think, 'Oh, so was that . . . and that.'"

so that she could grow more climbers. She began by adding a garage with a deck above and
engaging landscape designer Bill Harrison to
lay out the beds. A visit to France that included
a tour of Monet's garden inspired the trellises
that now define two sides of the back garden.
Thanks to a handy tape measure, she was able
to measure Monet's famous green iron arches
and have her blue-grey wooden ones made to
the same dimensions. She chose vigorous ram-
blers 'Seagull' and 'Bobbie James', both white,
and 'Veilchenblau', a soft lavender with white
markings, to cover the one that spans the back
garden, and interplanted clematis to contribute
more colour after the roses finished blooming.
On the adjoining trellis, which runs alongside
the ditch, 'Albertine' and 'Galway Bay' delight
passersby with their profusion of pink flowers
in summer.

Beds in the garden enclosed by these trellises are filled with neatly spaced rosebushes,
each bed adhering to a particular colour theme.
Here and there, delphiniums and foxgloves add
their spires to the design, but there is no doubt
about where the focus of the garden lies.

In the front garden, more formal beds hold yet more
roses. Initially they were confined to a border surrounding a square of lawn, but as the katsura trees she had
planted on the boulevard grew larger and their roots invaded more of the rich soil in the beds, Janet gradually
dug up the lawn. It still remains but has effectively
traded places with the roses—where they once framed
it, it now frames them. In the neat rectangles that pattern its smooth surface, Janet indulges her love of
strong colour with hybrid tea roses in vibrant reds and
oranges, grouping three of each variety together to
make a more dazzling display. In the background, a scarlet climbing rose, 'Danse du Feu,' shoulders its way up

the house beside clematis 'Huldine', with a perennial
nicotiana of similar hue to clothe its bare canes at
ground level. Where steps lead up to the front door, another sturdy climber, 'Spanish Beauty,' rises out of a
dark corner, waving huge, frilled pink petals above the
railing. The path that leads from the road to the bottom
of the steps crosses the ditch under an arch hung with
Clematis viticella and another pink rose appropriately
named 'High Hopes'.

In the narrow passage between front and back gardens, more delicate roses soak up the sun that warms
the wall of the house, and a 'Christmas Cheer' rhododendron brightens the view from the windows each
spring. Where a driveway breaks the flow of plants, the

gap is bridged by 'Albéric Barbier', an old rambler whose vigorous canes twine over the entrance to the garage and frame it with clusters of pale yellow blossoms in summer. One of Janet's favourite roses, an early hybrid tea called 'Mrs. Oakley Fisher', grows in an angle between ditch and drive. A large shrub, it draws exclamations from passing strangers when its delicate petals, the colour of a pastel sunset, unfold around a tuft of burgundy stamens.

Other, even older shrub roses fill some of the awkward spaces under trees and in shadier corners. When they flower in June, their fragrance carries on the air, and in winter they brighten the garden with sprays of vermilion hips. Janet particularly likes combining them with clematis, and many of her 30 or so varieties of the vine wind among their thorny branches. She finds that the colours of both plants blend well together, although she has chosen most of the clematis to flower earlier or later than the roses, so it isn't often an issue.

Plants other than roses are frequently gifts from friends or old favourites that have travelled with her from house to house over the years as cuttings. Impatiens, polyantha primulas and tuberous begonias came with her from Vancouver Island and from West Point Grey before that. Lilies, peonies and iris are more recent acquisitions. With a cottage nursery across the street and one of Vancouver's most popular garden centres a few blocks away, temptation is always at hand.

For her roses, though, Janet sends to England or orders from a wholesaler through the Vancouver Rose Society, of which she is a past president. In an average year, she will order 30 new roses, making room for them by ousting varieties that have not lived up to their promise. A few years ago she confided to friends that she was planning to cut back, maybe introduce some low-maintenance shrubs like hydrangeas because "the garden is getting older, and so am I." This season, to no one's surprise, there were 50 roses on her order form. ℭℱ

WATERFRONT HOTEL HERB GARDEN

"The primary focus is on use in the kitchen, so we aim to combine the decorative with the practical."

—ELAINE STEVENS

AROUND CANADA PLACE ON THE edge of Vancouver's harbour, the choice suites in most of the gleaming glass and steel high-rise hotels look across the water towards the North Shore mountains. However, the third floor of the Waterfront Hotel offers guests another option—a south-facing room opening onto a 2,100-square-foot herb garden, the brainchild of executive chef Daryle Ryo Nagata and gardener/herbalist Elaine Stevens.

Laid out in traditional style and separated by narrow gravel paths, the geometric beds edged with box, santolina and lavender contain all the usual culinary herbs as well as lesser-known Oriental delicacies and a range of edible flowers. Plants grow in a layer of earth three feet deep on the roof of the long hall and vestibule that faces onto busy Water Street. As Elaine Stevens explains, "it is like being on top of a heating pad, so everything is

way ahead of a regular garden."

Year-round herbs include chives, both regular and garlic varieties, and a bed of assorted thymes, silver leaves blending with golden and green ones in a nubbly, undulating mat. French tarragon and rosemary share another rectangle, and a sturdy border of grey-leaved *Santolina* contains the natural exuberance of various mints.

Among the more unusual plants are perennial arugula (*Eruca vesicaria*) and *Stevia rabaudiana*, a native of Paraguay whose spearmint-shaped leaves have the sweetness and granular texture of sugar, for which it is a herbal substitute. Gotu kola (*Centella asiatica*), a pot herb renowned in the Orient for its regenerative properties, and true marshmallow (*Althea officinalis*) grow here, too, among low clumps of salad burnet and tall fronds of fennel.

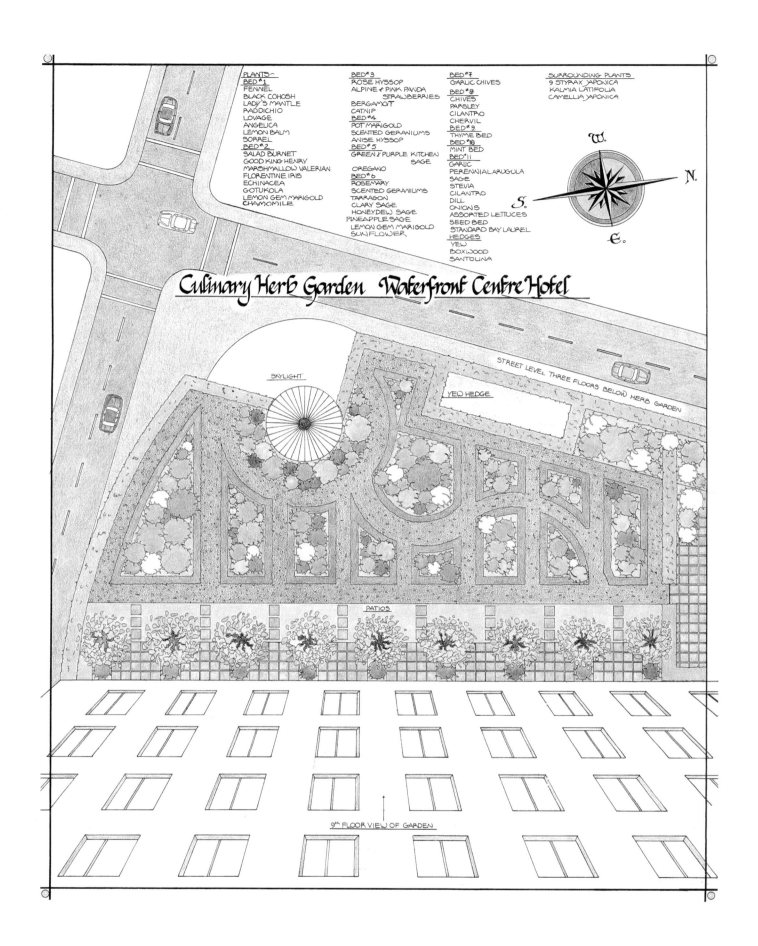

PLANTS~
BED #1
FENNEL
BLACK COHOSH
LADY'S MANTLE
RADDICHIO
LOVAGE
ANGELICA
LEMON BALM
SORREL
BED #2
SALAD BURNET
GOOD KING HENRY
MARSHMALLOW VALERIAN
FLORENTINE IRIS
ECHINACEA
GOTUKOLA
LEMON GEM MARIGOLD
CHAMOMILE

BED #3
ROSE HYSSOP
ALPINE & PINK PANDA
           STRAWBERRIES
BERGAMOT
CATNIP
BED #4
POT MARIGOLD
SCENTED GERANIUMS
ANISE HYSSOP
BED #5
GREEN & PURPLE KITCHEN
            SAGE
OREGANO
BED #6
ROSEMARY
SCENTED GERANIUMS
TARRAGON
CLARY SAGE
HONEYDEW SAGE
PINEAPPLE SAGE
LEMON GEM MARIGOLD
SUNFLOWER

BED #7
GARLIC CHIVES
BED #8
CHIVES
PARSLEY
CILANTRO
CHERVIL
BED #9
THYME BED
BED #10
MINT BED
BED #11
GARLIC
PERENNIAL ARUGOLA
SAGE
STEVIA
CILANTRO
DILL
ONIONS
ASSORTED LETTUCES
SEED BED
STANDARD BAY LAUREL
HEDGES
YEW
BOXWOOD
SANTOLINA

SURROUNDING PLANTS
9 STYRAX YAPONICA
KALMIA LATIFOLIA
CAMELLIA YAPONICA

W.
N.
S.
E.

Culinary Herb Garden Waterfront Centre Hotel

SKYLIGHT

STREET LEVEL THREE FLOORS BELOW HERB GARDEN

YEW HEDGE

PATIOS

9TH FLOOR VIEW OF GARDEN

"Growing herbs in my own garden allows me the opportunity to personalize every meal — from the planting of the seeds to the last garnish on the plate." –Daryle Ryo Nagata

There is even a section devoted to teas, so that the kitchen can provide guests with pots of tea made from freshly dried chamomile, bergamot and lemon balm, as well as the familiar mint.

Small birds flutter and chirp among leafy stems of dahlias and marigolds, grown for their decorative edible petals, and scatter seeds from the heads of sunflowers and echinacea. The hotel staff are proud of their part in providing a downtown haven for these little creatures, although their presence also prompts occasional visits from a peregrine falcon, equally appreciative of a meal.

In one corner of the garden, a domed skylight rising over the hall below is surrounded by a hedge of roses with simple flowers of creamy white, brushmarked in pink. The unsprayed petals are used in desserts, and, later in the year, oval orange hips provide a basis for teas.

A standard bay tree in a sea of green basil also contributes height to the composition, and Elaine has plans to add a row of dwarf apples to screen the garden from the hotel swimming pool which flanks its western edge. The railings that enclose the garden are disguised by carefully clipped yew hedges, interspersed along the street edge with neat clumps of *Pieris japonica* for colour interest.

While the emphasis is on fresh herbs, one of the larger beds in the garden is reserved for vegetables. Root crops in winter, leafy greens in summer come from this small plot, its contents ever-changing not just with the seasons but also with Elaine's experimental spirit.

The hotel sets aside one evening a month for a dinner highlighting the use of the garden's produce. The four-course meal is preceded by a tour of the herb beds conducted by Daryle and Elaine, and guests go home with instructions on how to duplicate the dishes in their own kitchens. Those who choose to stay overnight may find more reminders of this unusual garden in their bedrooms—sprigs of lavender tucked among the pillows. ❧

TRUDY DIXON'S GARDEN

"The shade garden is not hugely colourful, which pleases me —
every flower gets to be a prima donna."

WHERE THE WATERS ALONG THE shore of West Vancouver get chopped into rough little waves by winds blowing off the Strait of Georgia, properties are long and narrow, recoiling from the elements under a bulwark of ragged firs and wide-spreading deciduous shade trees. In the narrow lanes that lead to these hideaways, neighbours take their weekend strolls in a deceptive country calm.

From Trudy Dixon's black wrought-iron gate, you can look down on a narrow winding stone path disappearing out of sight under a canopy of copper beeches. Shafts of sunlight filtering through carefully trimmed laurels pick out the veining on the leaves of hostas, ferns and wands of Solomon's seal. "I'm good at pruning," Trudy Dixon says, as she points out how the impenetrable hedge of laurel at the gate is here separated into single bushes to

allow that play of golden light over the drifts of green foliage.

Where there is bloom, it is subtle – small, pale flowers of hardy geraniums, dark purple stars of *Clematis* 'Etoile Violette', greenish-white teardrops on the stems of the Solomon's seal. On the walls of a small studio, a climbing rose, 'Madame Alfred Carrière', pushes a few pearl pink flowers high up into the gable. A *Cornus kousa* adds a blanket of creamy flowers in spring and a subtle touch of rosy colour in fall. Around the corner, the white clusters of another rose, 'Bobbie James', garland a side wall in mid-summer, its sturdy canes springing from a half-barrel that restrains its usual rampant growth. This confinement is a necessity, not a choice, because the garden is on solid rock: Trudy has to fight for soil wherever she hopes to plant.

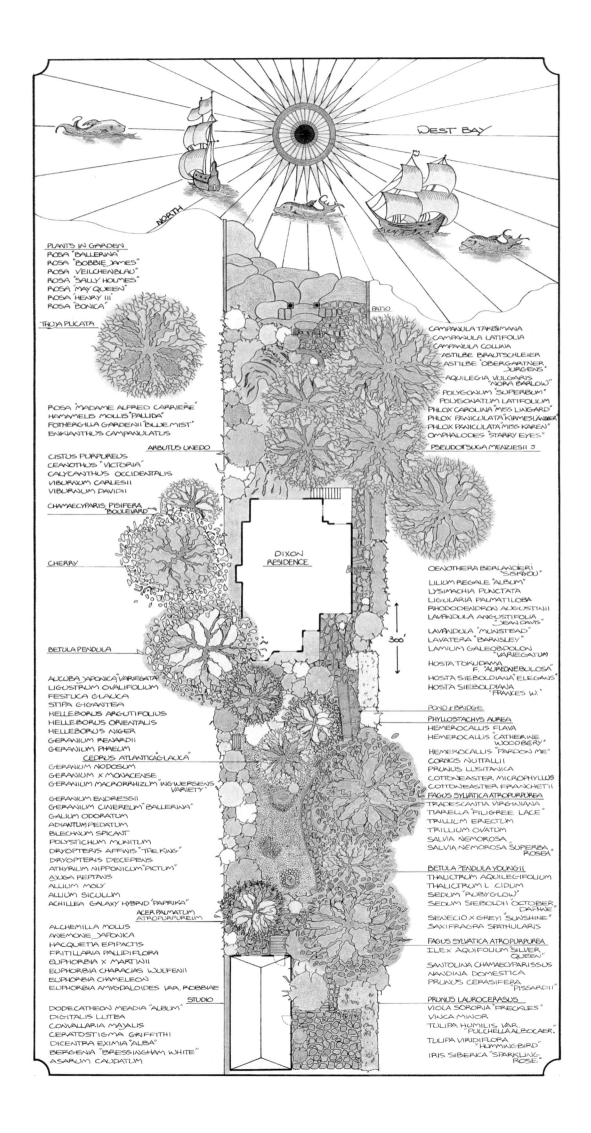

WEST BAY

NORTH

PLANTS IN GARDEN
ROSA "BALLERINA"
ROSA "BOBBIE JAMES"
ROSA "VEILCHENBLAU"
ROSA "SALLY HOLMES"
ROSA "MAY QUEEN"
ROSA "HENRY III"
ROSA "BONICA"

THUYA PLICATA

ROSA "MADAME ALFRED CARRIÈRE"
HAMAMELIS MOLLIS "PALLIDA"
FOTHERGILLA GARDENII "BLUE MIST"
ENKIANTHUS CAMPANULATUS

ARBUTUS UNEDO

CISTUS PURPUREUS
CEANOTHUS "VICTORIA"
CALYCANTHUS OCCIDENTALIS
VIBURNUM CARLESII
VIBURNUM DAVIDII

CHAMAECYPARIS PISIFERA
"BOULEVARD"

CHERRY

DIXON
RESIDENCE

BETULA PENDULA

AUCUBA JAPONICA "VARIEGATA"
LIGUSTRUM OVALIFOLIUM
FESTUCA GLAUCA
STIPA GIGANTEA
HELLEBORUS ARGUTIFOLIUS
HELLEBORUS ORIENTALIS
HELLEBORUS NIGER
GERANIUM RENARDII
GERANIUM PHAEUM
CEDRUS ATLANTICA GLAUCA
GERANIUM NODOSUM
GERANIUM X MONACENSE
GERANIUM MACRORRHIZUM "INGWERSEN'S
VARIETY"
GERANIUM ENDRESSII
GERANIUM CINEREUM "BALLERINA"
GALIUM ODORATUM
ADIANTUM PEDATUM
BLECHNUM SPICANT
POLYSTICHUM MUNITUM
DRYOPTERIS AFFINIS "THE KING"
DRYOPTERIS DECEPENS
ATHYRIUM NIPPONICUM "PICTUM"
AJUGA REPTANS
ALLIUM MOLY
ALLIUM SICULUM
ACHILLEA GALAXY HYBRID "PAPRIKA"
ACER PALMATUM
ATROPURPUREUM
ALCHEMILLA MOLLIS
ANEMONE JAPONICA
HACQUETIA EPIPACTIS
FRITILLARIA PALLIDIFLORA
EUPHORBIA X MARTINII
EUPHORBIA CHARACIAS WULFENII
EUPHORBIA CHAMELEON
EUPHORBIA AMYGDALOIDES VAR. ROBBIAE

STUDIO

DODECATHEON MEADIA "ALBUM"
DIGITALIS LUTEA
CONVALLARIA MAJALIS
CERATOSTIGMA GRIFFITHI
DICENTRA EXIMIA "ALBA"
BERGENIA "BRESSINGHAM WHITE"
ASARUM CAUDATUM

PATIO

CAMPANULA TAKESIMANA
CAMPANULA LATIFOLIA
CAMPANULA COLLINA
ASTILBE BRAUTSCHLEIER
ASTILBE "OBERGAARTNER
JÜRGENS"
AQUILEGIA VULGARIS
"NORA BARLOW"
POLYGONUM "SUPERBUM"
POLYGONATUM LATIFOLIUM
PHLOX CAROLINA "MISS LINGARD"
PHLOX PANICULATA "KIRMESLÄNDER"
PHLOX PANICULATA "MISS KAREN"
OMPHALODES "STARRY EYES"

PSEUDOTSUGA MENZIESII 5

OENOTHERA BERLANDIERI
"SISKIYOU"
LILIUM REGALE "ALBUM"
LYSIMACHIA PUNCTATA
LIGULARIA PALMATILOBA
RHODODENDRON AUGUSTINII
LAVANDULA ANGUSTIFOLIA
"JEAN DAVIS"
LAVANDULA "MUNSTEAD"
LAVATERA "BARNSLEY"
LAMIUM GALEOBDOLON
"VARIEGATUM"
HOSTA TOKUDAMA
F. "AUREONEBULOSA"
HOSTA SIEBOLDIANA "ELEGANS"
HOSTA SIEBOLDIANA
"FRANCES W."

POND & BRIDGE

PHYLLOSTACHYS AUREA
HEMEROCALLIS FLAVA
HEMEROCALLIS "CATHERINE
WOODBERY"
HEMEROCALLIS "PARDON ME"
CORNUS NUTTALLII
PRUNUS LUSITANICA
COTONEASTER MICROPHYLLUS
COTONEASTER FRANCHETII
FAGUS SYLVATICA ATROPURPUREA
TRADESCANTIA VIRGINIANA
TIARELLA "FILIGREE LACE"
TRILLIUM ERECTUM
TRILLIUM OVATUM
SALVIA NEMOROSA
SALVIA NEMOROSA "SUPERBA
ROSEA"

BETULA PENDULA YOUNGII
THALICTRUM AQUILEGIFOLIUM
THALICTRUM LUCIDUM
SEDUM "RUBYGLOW"
SEDUM SIEBOLDII "OCTOBER
DAPHNE"
SENECIO X GREYI "SUNSHINE"
SAXIFRAGA SPATHULARIS

FAGUS SYLVATICA ATROPURPUREA
ILEX AQUIFOLIUM "SILVER
QUEEN"
SANTOLINA CHAMAECYPARISSUS
NANDINA DOMESTICA
PRUNUS CERASIFERA
"PISSARDII"

PRUNUS LAUROCERASUS
VIOLA SORORIA "FRECKLES"
VINCA MINOR
TULIPA HUMILIS VAR.
PULCHELLA ALBOCAER.
TULIPA VIRIDIFLORA
"HUMMINGBIRD"
IRIS SIBERICA "SPARKLING
ROSE"

300'

"To me, even if you didn't see any more of the garden than this view as you enter, it would be enough."

Looking out across the garden from this point, with the path curving away to the right, your gaze wanders across a scree of mottled grey pebbles, past a group of small azaleas huddled against an island of lava rock and comes to rest on a distant wooden bench in a small clearing. Beside it, a spark of red glowing among the green foliage belongs to the rayed petals of a tiny dahlia. Trudy loves the scene, especially the impact of the single flower, or the flicker of colour and movement that occurs when one of her young granddaughters or a cat crosses the pool of pale sunshine—"like opening a door onto a magical world."

Behind the bench, two 'Arpege' azaleas mimic the dapple with their soft yellow flowers in May, and a *Calycanthus occidentalis* arches overhead, its curious ochre and dusty red flowers casting their spicy scent on the air in June.

All along the edge of the garden a thick groundcover

of hellebores, geraniums, meadow rue, *Astrantia major* and *Campanula takesimana* is backed by an equally dense curtain of bamboo, viburnum and cotoneaster.

Where the path curves, the long fingers of a weeping birch sweep to the ground. Beneath their shelter, a mossy nook cradles trilliums and ferns. The massive, grey-skinned trunks of the copper beeches to either side are shadowed with patterns of lichen and scrolled with ivy. Tiny ferns cling like green starfish to the moss at their feet. It is very quiet and very still, the only movement a play of dancing light over moss and pebbles, the only sound a whisper of falling leaves and a few needles dropping from a blue Atlas cedar.

The approach to the house crosses a rustic wooden bridge over a pool of black water, goldfish gleaming here and there in its depths, an occasional dragonfly skimming the surface. Near the door clusters of pots and troughs hold herbs, sedums and a few small flowering perennials. "You can't see much of the garden from inside the house," says Trudy, "so I like to make little groupings to look out at from the kitchen or the breakfast table."

An *Aucuba japonica* 'Variegata' dominates the bed adjoining the small entry deck. Trudy admits to disliking its yellow-splashed leaves at first, but has adapted to it by continuing the theme of green and gold in the surrounding plants, which include *Hamamelis mollis* 'Pallida' and *Clematis orientalis*. The experience has taught her to appreciate how the right companions can turn ugly ducklings into swans.

Clematis are favourite plants and, apart from the rhododendrons which pre-date Trudy's arrival, provide the majority of colour in the garden. Behind the aucuba, a mass of *Clematis chrysocoma* scales a cedar, and one of the evergreen varieties stretches over the narrow path that leads around the western side of the house. On the eastern side, where a deeper gloom prevails, shrubby *Clematis heracleifolia* in terracotta pots brightens dim corners with its flowers like scraps of bleached blue denim, and the tendrils of *Clematis* 'Madame Julia Correvon', 'Kermesina' and 'Jackmanii' crawl over the surface of azaleas, stringing them with stars of deep crimson and dusky purple when their own bright blooms have gone.

These cool passages are continuations of the leafy glade behind the house, so it is all the more exhilarating to emerge from their dimness into a brisk, salty air that crisps the grass and sands the boulders smooth along the water's edge. Five tall Douglas firs brace themselves against the wind, their trunks rising 20 feet high before spreading shaggy arms as if for balance. Below them, a shelf of grey rock breaks through the earth like the back of a whale, crusted with barnacles of *Sedum* 'Capo Blanco' and tufts of blue oat grass.

Above the shoreline, clumps of salt-resistant, grey-leaved plants — lavender, senecio and rock rose — blend their warmer tones with the rocks and mingle their blue and pink flowers with the petals of pale pink 'Bonica' roses. Two huge strawberry trees (*Arbutus unedo*) shelter the garden on the northeast side. Even in the calm of a late summer day, it is a dramatic landscape of earth, sea and sky, as quintessentially west coast as the deep stillness of the woodland a few steps away. ❧

MAUREEN LUNN'S GARDEN

"We wanted the feeling of the land embracing us."

FROM THE ROAD THAT LOOPS along the top of the hillside above Spanish Banks, the view is of a landscape under strict control. The strip of boulevard is an immaculate sheet of emerald grass, tightly clipped and laser-level. Behind it a dark hedge of holly, straight as a plumb line, is underplanted with a lighter ribbon of *Epimedium × rubrum.*

So it is surprising to find, on the other side of that hedge, the informality of a woodland garden flanking a sinuous S-curve of gravel drive. Within a border of yew hedge as rigid as the holly, billows of smooth, fat hosta leaves wash up against spiky clumps of *Ligularia przewalskii* and eddy around the base of mahonias, rhododendrons and white-trunked birches. Colour comes from the rhododendron flowers in spring fol-

lowed by the golden spears of the ligularia and later by drifts of pink Japanese anemones. The drive makes its final turn around the graceful silhouette of an old apple tree and widens into a broad rectangular parking area dominated by the facade of the house, a long weighty wall of pale ochre.

The only evidence of an entry is a sliver of an opening off-centre in the wall. Above it, a spar of cedar-slatted roofing stabs out into the courtyard, while on either side asymmetrical bronze planters lean towards each other, planted with tree ferns so huge that you can look up at the pattern of brown spores on their undersides as you pass beneath.

Inside, smooth slabs of stone make a path to the door across an open courtyard. On the right there is just

room for a small square pool brimming with water. On the left, the overflow emerges from beneath your feet and spills down a series of sandstone wedges until it seemingly disappears under the glass wall of the living-room below. Two maples, *Acer palmatum* 'Oregon Sunset', occupy ledges at different levels in this spare landscape, and provide a fine russet veil through which, from the bottom of the falls, you can look up to a circle of red cedar trunks telescoping inwards as they climb towards a distant circle of sky. All this green and bronze overhead is mirrored in an underplanting of pelargoniums in similar tones, interspersed with *Heuchera* 'Palace Purple' and *Coleus* 'The Line', which has a vein of matching purple down the centre of each lime green leaf. Trails of jasmine fall, in imitation of the water, down one pale terracotta wall.

The low-slung bulk of the house almost spans the width of the property and disguises the steepness of the drop from entry level to a broad apron of smooth green lawn on the far side. Glass curtain walls under deep eaves provide an almost seamless transition from indoor to outdoor space, helped by continuation of the stone floor across a wide patio right to the neat edge of grass. In fact, the shift is subtle enough that at least one dinner guest has walked unawares into a pane of glass.

"When I plant, I often make my decisions by looking out from inside the house," Maureen says. In the early stages, she enlisted the help of Nenagh McCutcheon, a designer with the well-known Rule, Sangha and Associates company, to create a design that would stand up to the strong lines of the house, but it was Dan White, the architect of the house, who suggested the striking feature that draws all eyes at first sight . . .

At the far edge of the lawn, a semicircle of perennial border, punctuated with geysers of ornamental grasses,

backs up against a protective screen of huge firs and cedars on the edge of Pacific Spirit Park. Tumbling towards it across the seamless green surface is a row of giant sandstone dominoes, the nearer ones upright, the farthest flat in the grass. So dramatic is its effect that it temporarily eclipses the other, more subtle elements of the landscape.

And subtlety is what the planting here is all about. Although Maureen Lunn admits to loving the interweaving colours of European borders, she recognizes that "they wouldn't work here" and has turned instead towards combinations of texture and form. An artist who creates intricate collages of found objects like shells, leaves, stones and fragments of driftwood in her on-site studio, she has applied the same talents to the larger composition of her garden, using grasses, ferns, hostas and other bold-leafed plants as elements in a living pattern. Silky fronds of *Miscanthus sinensis* contrast with blades of iris and daylily leaves, jagged teeth of ferns, and swaying stems of Japanese anemones. Although flashes of colour come in different seasons as rhododendron flowers are followed by roses and later

by the daylilies and anemones, the greens, blues and occasional purples of foliage predominate.

Close to the house, Maureen has filled a rectangular bed with blue-leafed succulents: sedums and sempervivums, agaves and euphorbias. Her original plan was to have a thyme garden here, but, as the herb was losing the battle with an invasion of moss while the succulents flourished, she let the latter have their way.

Around the corner, a small barbecue area also acts as a holding area for plants she buys "because I wonder what they look like," as well as more practical things like lettuce and strawberries. Under the wide eaves of the house, the earth is so dry that little will grow except ivy, although Maureen has been pleasantly surprised to find that hostas will tolerate it, too.

On the far side of the lawn behind a screen of vine maples, Maureen's studio balances on the very edge of a ravine, looking out into a forest of ivy-clad alders and big-leaf maples. The broad shallow steps that lead down to it cleave through a sea of ferns. Sharp blades of *Crocosmia* 'Lucifer' and chartreuse flowers of *Nicotiana langsdorfii* play variations on the green theme, while later in the year the brilliant red blooms of 'Lucifer' will anticipate the fall colours of the vine maples.

House and studio are visually linked by a long strip of blue water that runs along one side of the lawn. Both the Lunns were competitive swimmers and this Olympic-length lap pool allows them to keep up their prowess while adding a unique element to the composition of the garden. A low wall on the far side of the pool is festooned with *Escallonia* 'Newport Dwarf' and *Senecio greyi*. When both are in flower, their hot pink and golden flowers respectively, combined with the azure water, create a real-life interpretation of a David Hockney painting.

At the end of the pool beside the house, the land rises steeply towards the entry court. A small path climbs the bank, dappled with sunlight shining through a canopy

of katsura trees, and provides a view down to a piece of angular modern sculpture in a square of shallow water. The glass wall of the house encloses one side of the square. On the others, a recent planting of 150 *Taxus repens* fills the tiers that zigzag up and out from the pool below like hard-edged, square ripples. It is a bold planting, clean and monochromatic, much as the house is, relying on shape and mass rather than detail for its effect.

This use of planes in the architecture of both house and garden stands up well to the surrounding forest, acknowledging the tall silhouettes of fir and cedar that dominate the landscape and matching them with a grandeur and spare beauty of its own that is very much of this time and this place. ℰ

PAGE 184
Leaves of *Acer palmatum* 'Oregon Sunset' are silhouetted against slabs of rosy sandstone.

PAGE 185
A sunny corner holds pots of carnations, grasses and strawberries.

PAGE 187
Steps to the studio are shaded by vine maples and lined with ferns.

PAGE 188
Shade-loving *Rodgersia aesculifolia, Ligularia przewalskii* and hostas line the driveway.

PAGE 189
The lap pool and lawn echo the architecture with their broad blocks of colour.

INDEX OF PLANTS
FEATURED IN PHOTOGRAPHS

Hydrangea
   H. 'Blue Wave', 47, 83
   H. 'Soeur Therese', 109
   H. macrophylla , 45
   H. serrata 'Bluebird', 68

Impatiens, 98, 136, 141
Iris, 97, 154
Ivy, 44, 103, 116
   Hedera colchica 'Dentata Variegata', 48–49
   Hedera helix 'Glacier', 80

Japanese cutleaf maple, 54–55, 56, 97
Japanese maple, 54–55, 56, 97
Juniper, 152

Kirengeshoma palmata, 73

Lady's mantle (Alchemilla mollis), 13
Lambs' ears (Stachys byzantina), 65
Laurel, 11
Laurentia axillaris, 129
Lavandula stoechas, 114
Lavatera 'Barnsley', 81
Lavender, 81
Leopard's bane (Doronicum orientale), 95
Leucothoe fontanesiana, 38
Lichen, 151
Ligularia, 188
Ligustrum japonicum 'Texanum', 115
Lobelia, 127

Magnolia, 59
Marigold 'Lemon Gem', 175
Medusa, 111
Monkey puzzle tree (Araucaria araucana), 130

Ornamental cabbages 'Red Pigeon' and 'White pigeon', 87

Pansies, 165
Pelargonium, 161
Pennisetum setaceum 'Rubrum', 146
Petasites japonicus, 137
Petunias, 86
Picea abies, 179
Pieris japonica, 99
Pine, 23
Polystichum munitum, 38
Prunus 'Mount Fuji'
Prunus × yedoensis, 28–29
Pulmonaria officinalis, 48–49

Rhododendron, 50, 59, 93, 97
   R. cinnabarinum, 97
   R. impeditum, 63

Robinia pseudoacacia 'Frisia', 43, 67
Rodgersia aesculifolia, 188
Rose
   R. 'American Pillar', 170–1
   R. 'Complicata', 104
   R. Electron', 167
   R. 'F.J. Grootendorst', 89
   R. 'Iceberg', 71
   R. 'Elina', 47
   R. 'Graham Thomas', 84
   R. longicuspis
   R. 'Mary Rose', 171
   R. 'Paul Lédé', 74
   R. 'Queen Elizabeth', 86
   R. 'Seagull', 166, 170–1
   R. 'The Fairy', 109
   R. 'Veilchenblau', 166, 170–1
Rosemary, 110

Sage, 175
Santolina, 176
Sedum, 78
   S. 'Autumn Joy', 57, 110
   S. spectabile
   S. telephium
Sempervivum tectorum, 78
Sequoiadendron giganteum 'Pendulum', 120–1
Shirley poppies, 81
Siberian iris (Iris sibirica), 148
Strawberries, 189
Swan River daisy, 127

Threadleaf cypress (Chamaecyparis pisifera 'Filifera Aurea'), 98
Thyme, 13
Tiger lilies, 136
Trachycarpus fortunei, 113
Tsuga canadensis 'Pendula', 139
Tulipa clusiana chrysantha, 165

Viburnum opulus, 73
Vine maple (Acer circuratum), 187
Violet, 69

Waterlily, 62
Weeping beech (Fagus sylvatica Pendula), 51
Western red cedar (Thuja plicta), 18
Willow, 27, 92
Willow-leafed pear (Pyrus salicifolia pendula), 32
Windmill palms (Trachycarpus fortunei), 131
Wisteria, 89, 92, 115
   W. sinensis alba, 35, 89
Witch hazel (Hamamelis mollis), 97

Yucca, 113

ACKNOWLEDGEMENTS

CHRISTINE ALLEN WISHES TO THANK: Mark Stanton, publisher emeritus of Raincoast Books and true believer; Brian Scrivener, Elaine Jones and Carolyn Jones, editors extraordinaire; Michal Kluckner, constant companion and first, best critic, and the gardeners—the words are mine but the vision belongs to them.

COLLIN VARNER WISHES TO ADD THANKS to Garth Ramsey, Terri Clark, Jack McKinnon and Wendy Varner.